To- Stacey,
Best wishes, may
you find a lot of
the wonderful toys
featured in this book.
Dottie Ayers
8-7-93

Advertising Art Of Steiff

Teddy Bears & Playthings

**Compiled By
Dottie Ayers &
Donna Harrison**

Translated by Lydia Pauli, M.D.

Published by Hobby House Press

Cumberland,
Maryland 21502

FOREWORD

In the early 1900s a popular German publication entitled *Illustrirte Zeitung* was found in most German households. This illustrated newspaper carried a wide range of advertisements from machinery, medicines, cameras, crackers, girdles and automobiles to Steiff stuffed toys. The Steiff ads, some in color, but mostly in black and white, dominated the newspaper with their designs and creativity. The following is a collection of those ads which appeared over the years 1911, 1912, 1913, 1914, 1925, 1928 and 1929. As you look through these ads, you will notice a lot of old familiar faces. In some, prices are listed for the items shown in German marks. In 1913 one mark was worth approximately $.24 in U.S. gold dollars, which made the now very rare *Golliwog* sell for only $.57. Before we run out to get a time machine to recapture those low prices, we must remember that an average weekly salary in the U.S. at that time was $17.* At the back of the book we have included a selection of our favorite postcards and photographs collected over the years. The dates are indicated where the postmarks could be detected.

* Based on six-day work week, *1913 Old World Almanac.*

Dottie Ayers
&
Donna Harrison

PART ONE
1913

DEAR, DEAR
FATHER CHRISTMAS!

As overheard from the nursery by Georg Queri

Lisbeth: Mama, when I write to Father Christmas, can I have Ami lick the stamp?

Max: Oh, Mama, if I am ever a traveler in Africa, then can the lions lick my stamps? I may catch a hundred lions.

Fritz: Then one of them may bite your fingers. A lion has teeth which are as long as a tree.

Lisbeth: Mama, do the elephants bite too? I would like to have an elephant who cannot bite and has a trunk all the way in the front. One will have to hang a little bell under the trunk so the flies can hear when he comes and say, "AHA, here comes the fat elephant!" Now we have to run away from him.

Max: Father Christmas also has a pretty monkey which has a trunk in the back. I want a monkey who can climb.

Fritz: Let's play travelers in Africa. I will be an animal tamer who stares at the lions; then they will be quiet and wave their paws.

Lisbeth: You know, Mama, I wish to go also to Africa and teach the little black children to learn the ABCs. Father Christmas has to bring me a teacher and many little black children to learn.

Max: Yeah. But what if they are all man-eaters?

Lisbeth: Then I will have a policeman who has to forbid the man-eating. Also, I will have a soldier who can sit in the kitchen.

Fritz: Yes, Mama, then Minna does not have to cry in the kitchen anymore. I will show her the soldier who salutes and eats the sausage.

Max: When I travel in Africa I will have a ship and many soldiers. All ship soldiers are called sailors and as the ship goes to and fro, one becomes seasick.

Lisbeth: Most soldiers are in the military. The handsome soldiers are sometimes called lieutenants.

Max.

Lieber, lieber Weihnachtsmann!
Erlauschtes aus der Kinderstube von Georg Queri.

Moritz.

Lisbeth: Mama, wenn ich dem Weihnachtsmann schreibe, darf ich dann die Briefmarke auch vom Ami ablecken lassen?

Max: O, Mama, wenn ich einmal ein Afrikareisender bin, dann müssen mir die Löwen die Briefmarken ablecken. Ich will hundert Löwen fangen.

Fritz: Dann beißt dich einer in die Finger. Ein Löwe hat Zähne, die sind so lang wie ein Baum.

Lisbeth: Mama, beißen die Elefanten auch? Ich möchte einen Elefanten haben, der nicht beißen kann und den Rüssel ganz vorne hat. Unten am Rüssel muß man ein Glöckchen anbinden, daß die Fliegen ihn gleich kommen hören und sagen: Aha, jetzt kommt der dicke Elefant! Jetzt müssen wir davonlaufen.

Max: Der Weihnachtsmann hat auch einen schönen Affen, der hat den Rüssel hinten. Ich will einen Affen haben, der klettern kann.

Fritz: Dann spielen wir Afrikareisender. Und

① Negerschule.

ich will einmal ein Tierbändiger werden, der schaut die Löwen nur so an, dann machen sie kusch und geben die Pfote.

Lisbeth: Weißt du, Mama, ich gehe auch nach Afrika und lerne den kleinen Negern das A B C. Und der Weihnachtsmann muß mir einen Lehrer schenken und viele kleine Negerlein.

Max: So, und wenn es aber lauter Menschenfresser sind?

Lisbeth: Ich will aber einen Schutzmann haben, der muß das Menschenfressen verbieten. Und einen Soldaten will ich auch haben, der darf in der Küche sitzen.

Fritz: Ja, Mama, dann muß die Minna nicht mehr weinen in der Küche. Ich will ihr den Soldaten zeigen, der macht Augen rechts und ißt die Wurst.

Max: Wenn ich einmal ein Afrikareisender bin, habe ich ein Schiff und viele Soldaten. Alle Soldaten heißt man Matrosen und das Schiff geht hin und her und wird seekrank.

Lisbeth: Beim Militär sind die meisten Soldaten. Die schönen Soldaten heißt man Leutnant.

Fritz: And when the lieutenant comes, the governess gets all red. The little black children never get red.

Max: But the Indians are always red. I would like to have an Indian who catches a bear. The bear grumbles and the Indian has to laugh.

Lisbeth: The soldiers on ships are called old seadogs. They have a pipe in their mouths which has to be lit. When they are not careful, the ship burns.

Max: Then comes the fire brigade and they are thirsty.

Fritz: Oh, Father Christmas's fire brigade is thirsty and one has a jug in which one has to put a lot of beer. When I go lion hunting, I will take with me a jug full of raspberry juice. It is very hot in Africa and the children have no jugs.

Lisbeth: In Africa there are monkeys which sit in a real cart and one of them pushes it.

Max: Father Christmas made the cart. The real monkeys sit on chocolate trees and eat them all up.

Fritz: The kangaroo has a great leather pouch in the belly and puts in it the chocolate for the little ones.

Lisbeth: I would also like to have a bear that is all white from eating all the snow.

Max: And when he has eaten a lot of snow, then his belly freezes and the Eskimo catches him.

Fritz: The Mrs. Eskimo pulls the fur from the bear and sews her children in it. When the child goes to school, the teacher runs away and brings a policeman.

Lisbeth: The policeman says, "You bad child; you have to come with me!"

Max: Yeah, and you must go to the circus, you bad child, and be real dumb.

Fritz: And the people say, "There is that dumb August."

Lisbeth: But there is a beautiful lady who dances on a horse and the people all wait for her to fall down!

Max: The Chinese in the circus don't fall down as they tie themselves in the air by their pigtail.

Fritz: In the circus there is a pig which when one pulls his tail, it says: "wee, wee." But the tail doesn't get any longer.

Lisbeth: And the camel stands there and is sad because he has two humps.

Max: But the camel in the zoo has one hump cut off.

Fritz: The most beautiful camel is a giraffe. It has a neck like a stork.

Lisbeth: I would like to have a stork, too. He has to bring me a lot of small babies.

Max: Babies are boring. The stork also brings small animals.

Fritz: But not always. Mama says Father brings small animals from the tavern. They are naughty, the little animals.

Lisbeth: Oh, I would like to have a pretty inn. There the farmers can sit and musicians play. There could be weddings in the inn.

Max: The bridegroom has a long nose and the bride has a beautiful dress and cries.

Fritz: Mama, why does the bride cry?

Lisbeth: When I am a bride, I will marry Father Christmas. Then I don't have to cry.

Max: Oh, Father Christmas is not really a man! Father Christmas is really a woman! Mama already mailed her letter yesterday to Margarete Steiff, Giengen a.d. Brenz.

① Tiertransport.

Fritz: Und wenn der Leutnant kommt, dann wird die Gouvernante rot. Die kleinen Negerlein werden nicht rot.

Max: Aber die Indianer sind immer rot. Ich möchte einen Indianer, der einen Bären fängt. Der Bär brummt, da muß der Indianer lachen.

Lisbeth: Die Soldaten auf den Schiffen heißt man Seebären. Sie haben eine Pfeife im Mund, die muß man anzünden. Wenn sie nicht Obacht geben, brennt das Schiff.

Max: Dann kommt die Feuerwehr und hat Durst.

Fritz: O, dem Weihnachtsmann seine Feuerwehr hat Durst und einer hat einen Maßkrug, da muß man viel Bier hineintun. Wenn ich auf die Löwenjagd gehe, nehme ich einen Maßkrug voll Himbeerlimonade mit. In Afrika ist es sehr heiß, weil die Neger keine Maßkrüge haben.

Lisbeth: In Afrika sind Affen, die sitzen in einem echten Wagen und einer schiebt.

② Rekord Peter.

Max: Aber den Wagen hat der Weihnachtsmann gemacht. Die echten Affen sitzen auf den Schokoladenbäumen und essen alles auf.

Fritz: Aber das Känguruh hat eine große Ledertasche am Bauch und steckt noch Schokolade für die Jungen ein.

Lisbeth: Ich will auch einen Bären haben, der ist ganz weiß von lauter Schneeessen.

Max: Und wenn er recht viel Schnee gegessen hat, dann erfriert sein Bauch und dann fängt ihn der Eskimo.

Fritz: Und die Frau Eskimo zieht dem Bären den Pelz ab und näht ihre Kinder hinein. Und dann kommt das Kind in die Schule und der Lehrer läuft davon und holt einen Schutzmann.

Lisbeth: Und der Schutzmann sagt: du böses Kind, du mußt mit!

Max: Ja, und du mußt in den Zirkus, du böses Kind, und recht dumm sein.

Fritz: Und die Leute sagen: das ist der dumme August.

Lisbeth: Aber eine schöne Dame, die tanzt auf einem Pferd und die Leute warten bis sie herunterfällt!

Max: Die Chinesen im Zirkus, die fallen nicht herunter, die binden sich mit dem Zopf in der Luft fest.

Fritz: Im Zirkus ist ein Schwein, das zieht einer am Schwanz, dann macht es: vivi, vivi. Aber der Schwanz wird nicht länger.

Lisbeth: Und das Kamel steht auch da und ist traurig, weil es zwei Höcker hat.

Max: Aber das Kamel im Zoo, dem haben sie einen Höcker weggeschnitten.

Fritz: Das schönste Kamel ist die Giraffe. Die hat einen Hals wie ein Storch.

Lisbeth: Ich will auch einen Storch haben. Der muß mir recht viele kleine Kinder bringen.

Max: Kleine Kinder sind langweilig. Der Storch bringt auch die kleinen Tiere.

Fritz: Aber nicht alle. Mama sagt, Papa bringt die kleinen Tiere aus dem Gasthaus mit, die sind pfui, die kleinen Tiere.

Lisbeth: Oh, ich möchte ein schönes Gasthaus haben! Da sitzen die Bauern, und die Musikanten müssen blasen. In den Gasthäusern ist Hochzeit.

Max: Der Bräutigam hat eine lange Nase und die Braut hat ein schönes Kleid und weint.

Fritz: Mama, warum weint denn die Braut?

Lisbeth: Wenn ich einmal Braut bin, heirate ich den Weihnachtsmann. Dann muß ich nicht weinen.

Max: Oh, der Weihnachtsmann ist ja gar kein Mann! Der Weihnachtsmann ist ja eine Frau! Die Mama hat gestern ihren Brief schon weggeschickt: An

Margarete Steiff
Giengen a. d. Brenz.

PART TWO
1911

① *From the cradle of our Lord.*
② *The last swig.*
③ *A feast for ears.*

THE CRADLE OF THE
TEDDY BEAR

The Americans alone did not invent the symbol of their affection for their Roosevelt. At the fair at Leipzig, the toy dealers say the funny little plush bear came from a little town in Württemberg and they added him with indifference to their toy stock. But overseas the jolly bear doll was liked and the old "Rough Rider" Roosevelt just recently brought the attention to bears with his grizzly bear hunt. Due to this, the toy became a national symbol overnight and became famous all over the world under the name of a teddy bear. The children all over the United States just had to have the plush bear, desiring him with all their heart. The ladies carried him tenderly on their arms and gentlemen exhibited him in their clubs. And so again there came the time when America had to put in large orders to the German toy industry. The small town of Giengen-on-the-Brenz became the central point of a line of toys for the New York toy buyers. As it happened, one million dollars of orders went to Giengen in 1907 besides the sums spent all over Germany for the fast-emerging imitations of their original toys.

The story of the teddy bear goes back 30 years. At that time, Miss Margarete Steiff used to sew small elephants with her skillful needle from the remnants of materials, stuffed them with wool and gave them as gifts to her female friends. The circle of her friends grew and Margarete sewed and sewed. It then occurred to her brother to show the pretty art of his sister at the nearby Heidenham market. In no time, the whole crate full of small cloth elephants, the jolly little animals, was sold out.

In the history of its highly developed arts and crafts culture, Württemberg must never forget the Steiff name. Margarete Steiff, who in her loving simplicity, invented the cloth toy, was joined by Richard Steiff, her nephew, who with a good eye and artistic training, caught onto his aunt's amateur handicraft and with a youthful fervor, looked for new horizons. He hated the stiff porcelain of the contemporary dolls and he forced soft felt in new forms, painted them and created funny, and sometimes grotesque, but lively and lovable dolls of the future. But the wig! The doll's hair from obstinate material! He envied the art from the Thürigen makers who gave their dolls fine miniature hair styles. But when children were given his dolls, they snatched the fuzzy hair of the new toys with shouts and pulled, tugged and combed. There was great rejoicing from the little ones. This hair would not pull out. The cloth doll could not be torn. The little arms could be moved in all directions and the little legs could not be maimed and did not become soft or loose. With a grin, the family father started to save money otherwise spent for the doll hospital.

Richard Steiff's father, who admired the skills of Margarete Steiff, started to forge plans for his son. To sculpt and fashion! And since Richard did learn to sculpt from models at the Art School in Stuttgart, an animal trainer from Hagenbeck came to school with his bear, his most beloved bear. Richard was enchanted with the plump, good-natured agility of the brown companion and entrusted the grotesque poses to the modeling clay. There were dozens of merry scenes from the life of a bear. Ten years later—but here we beg the reader to recapitulate the subject of teddy bear from the above writing.

DIE WIEGE DES TEDDY-BÄREN.

① „Aus unsres Herrgotts Blumengarten".

Die Amerikaner haben das Symbol ihrer Zuneigung zu ihrem Roosevelt nicht selbst erfunden. Ihre Playthingshändler sahen auf der Leipziger Messe den drolligen kleinen Plüsch-Bären, der aus einem württembergischen Städtchen kam, und nahmen ihn gleichgültig in ihr Spielzeuglager auf. Aber da die lustige Bärenpuppe drüben gefiel und da der alte „rough rider" Roosevelt gerade durch seine Grizzley-Jagden auf sie aufmerksam werden ließ, wurde aus dem Spielzeug über Nacht ein nationales Symbol, das unter dem Namen Teddy-Bär dann in der ganzen Welt berühmt wurde. Die Kinder der ganzen Vereinigten Staaten mußten den Plüsch-Bären in der Schatzkammer ihrer Kinderlust haben, die Damen trugen ihn zärtlich auf dem Arm und die Herren stellten ihn in ihren Klubzimmern auf. So war der Moment wieder gekommen, da Amerika der deutschen Spielzeugindustrie große Aufträge zu erteilen hatte. Für die Neu-Yorker Kommissionäre wurde das alte württembergische Städtlein Giengen an der Brenz ein Zentralpunkt der Spielwarenbranche und es ereignete sich, daß beispielsweise im Jahre 1907 eine runde Million Dollars nach Giengen floß, abgesehen von den Summen, die allerwärts in Deutschland für die schnell aufgetauchten Imitationen des Originalspielzeugs eingingen.

Die Geschichte vom Teddybären greift auf drei Jahrzehnte zurück. Damals pflegte Fräulein Gretle Steiff mit ihrer geschickten Nadel kleine Elefanten aus Stoffresten zu nähen, sie mit Wolle auszustopfen und ihren Freundinnen als Nadelkissen zu schenken. Es erwuchs ihr ein Heer von Freundinnen. Und Gretle nähte und nähte. Da fiel's ihrem Bruder ein, die hübschen Künste der Schwester auf dem nahen Heidenheimer Markt zu zeigen. Gleich eine Kiste voll der kleinen Stoffelefanten — die lustigen Tierchen waren im Nu vergriffen.

② „In den letzten Zügen"

Württemberg darf in der Geschichte seines hochentwickelten Kunstgewerbes den Namen Steiff nie vergessen. Zu Gretle Steiff, die in liebevoller Schlichtheit das Stoffspielzeug erfand, trat Richard Steiff, der Neffe, der mit feinem Blick und künstlerischer Schulung in Tantchens Amateurhandwerk eingriff und mit jugendlichem Eifer neue Ziele suchte. Er haßte das starre Porzellan der landläufigen Puppe und zwang den weichen Filz in neue Formen, bepinselte ihn und schuf ulkig und grotesk manchmal, aber lebendig und allerliebst die Puppe der Zukunft. Aber die Perücke! Das Puppenhaar aus widerspenstigem Material! Er beneidete die Thüringer um ihre Künste, die den Puppen die feinen Miniaturfrisuren gaben. Aber die Kinder, denen er seine Puppen brachte, griffen jauchzend in das „Wuschelhaar" des neuen Spielzeuges und zerrten und zogen und kämmten. Großer Jubel der Kleinen. Dieses Haar war ja nicht auszuzerren. Diese Stoffpuppe war ja nicht zu zerreißen. Diese Ärmchen konnte man nach allen Richtungen drehen, diese Füßchen konnte man schauerlich maltraitieren, sie wichen und wankten nicht. In dieser Zeit begann der brave Familienvater schmunzelnd die Groschen für die Puppenklinik zu sparen.

Richard Steiff's Vater hatte, da er die Geschicklichkeit Gretle Steiff's bewunderte, Pläne für den Sohn geschmiedet. Modellieren, modellieren! Und da Richard in der Stuttgarter Kunstgewerbeschule modellierte, war ein Tierbändiger von Hagenbeck gekommen, der mit seinen Bären auftrat, mit seinen allerliebsten Bären. Richard war entzückt von der plump-gemütlichen Behendigkeit der braunen Gesellen und vertraute ihre grotesken Stellungen der Modelliermasse an. Dutzende von lustigen Szenen aus dem Bärenleben. Zehn Jahre später — aber da bitten wir den Leser oben die Sache vom Teddy-Bär zu rekapitulieren.

③ „Ein Ohrenschmaus!"

① *What's that?*
② *"---Secret Service!"*
③ *"Clowning" design from painter Schlopsnies.*
④ *Rehearsal from Sarrasani circus. Design from artist Albert Schlopsnies.*

Success leads to invention. Why not put a voice in the bears' bodies? A small bellows with vibrating plates was invented. Teddy learned to growl lightheartedly. But because the experiments with the bellows could produce all kinds of voices from God's world, one had to create animals to go with the happy, natural voices. A muhuhu—and an ox was created—for screeching, a monkey; for barking, a dog; for braying, a donkey; for roaring, a lion. How the children rejoiced! They pulled the Giengen plush pig's ear—and see—it squealed!

So Giengen conquered the market and from the small workshop of the amateur seamstress, Margarete Steiff, grew the great Margarete Steiff factory which today employs 2000 workers and gradually took over the whole area of the toy industry. Dolls and animals—was there still anything new to create? The call for more art in the handicraft became intense all over Germany; it was bound to penetrate the field of the toy industry.

Richard Steiff, the founder of the company, and his brothers, Paul, Hugo and Otto, brooded and deliberated. Was it appropriate to transfer the humorous side of people to the toys? They took the risk. And so the village musicians, the schoolmaster and his boys, and all the country and city characters came to life. They brought nothing of the learned seriousness; in contrast to the earlier demands of teaching, they brought humor into the world of fantasy of the little ones—the most important factor of life in the period of time that one calls the "Century of the Child."

Then one day there came to the Giengen factory an artist from Munich who displayed his marionettes, toys for young and old, which he created in a leisurely mood.

① „Na nu?!"

② „— Dienstgeheimnis!"

③ „Clownerie". Entwurf von Kunstmaler Schlopsnies.

Auch der Erfolg macht erfinderisch. Warum diesen Bären nicht eine Stimme in die Leiber geben? Ein winziger Blasebalg mit Stimmplättchen wurde erfunden. Teddy lernte vergnüglich brummen. Aber da die Versuche mit dem Blasebalg Stimmen aus der ganzen lieben Herrgottswelt hören ließen, mußte man um der lustigen Naturtöne willen auch das Getier dazu schaffen. Ein Muhuhuu — der Ochse dazu entstand. Zum Gekreisch der Affe; zum Gebell der Hund; zum Eselsschrei der Esel; zum Gebrüll der Löwe. Wie die Kinder jauchzten! Sie zogen das Giengener Plüschschweinchen am Ohr — siehe da, es schrie!

So eroberte Giengen den Markt. Und aus der kleinen Werkstatt der Amateurschneiderin Gretle Steiff wurde die große Fabrik Margarete Steiff, die heute an zweitausend Arbeitskräfte beschäftigt und das ganze Gebiet der Spielwarenindustrie allmählich in ihr Programm aufgenommen hat. Puppen und Tiere — war noch

neues zu schaffen? Der Ruf nach mehr Kunst im Handwerk war in ganz Deutschland mächtig geworden; er mußte auch in das Getriebe der Spielwaren - Industrie hineindringen. Richard Steiff, der Konstrukteur der Firma, und seine Brüder Paul, Hugo und Otto grübelten und sannen. War's angebracht, den Humor, der in den Leuten steckte, auf das Spielzeug zu übertragen? Sie riskierten. Und so entstanden die Dorfmusikanten, der Schulmeister und seine Buben und alle die Typen von Land und Stadt. Sie brachten nichts von belehrendem Ernste; gegenüber den Forderungen von frühestem Anschauungsunterricht brachten sie Humor in die Phantasiewelt der Kleinen, den wichtigsten Lebensfaktor in einer Zeit, die man „das Jahrhundert des Kindes" nennt. — Und eines Tages kam ein Münchner Künstler in die Giengener Fabrik und zeigte seine Marionettenfiguren, Spielzeuge für Klein und

④ „Probe im Zirkus Sarrasani". Entwurf von Kunstmaler Albert Schlopsnies.

Richard Steiff hired this man for his factory. This was not just anyone from the Munich School; it was Albert Schlopsnies, a young East Prussian, whose teacher was Franz Stuck.

One tells no tales out-of-school when one relates the evolution of this young painter. He was stuck in the store of his uncle, deep in East Prussia, very unhappy, scrawling on every piece of paper, begging for a future as an artist. In vain! So he took his bicycle and rode from Tilsit all the way to Munich. Franz Stuck, to whom he showed his drawings, learned about the above and took the talented artist as his pupil. Because of his master's pronounced interests, the pupil found pleasure in the artistic crafts. In Giengen, where he felt challenged, his natural talent awakened. Anyone who knows "Schwalangsher"—the name the Munich "Chevauxleger" gives himself, appreciates the cheerful artistic creations of the town porter, the dairy farmer and the farmers from the Steiff factory. A colorful crowd of jolly figures wanders through the menagerie of childhood's toy wonders: the clowns, the musicians, the jugglers, the servants, the Chinese and the Singhales and the dear public mingle with the colossal number of tamable, well-drilled Steiff animals.

The great toy enterprises and the great stores made use of the circus and similar extensive groups of the Giengen doll world for their window dressing. They drove Father Christmas to a collecting mania. Every year he puts the wonderful seven gifts under the Christmas tree and hopes that the Christ child will bring some more. Always more and more. And always new and beautiful. The passion of the creator added costly additions to the dolls in that he

① „Mein Liebling".

② „Die Dorfschule".

③ „Meister Petz als Reittier".

④ Pantom-Tiere.

⑤ „Auf Dickhäuters Rücken".

Groß, wie er sie in müßiger Laune gefertigt hatte. Richard Steiff gewann den Mann für die Firma. Er hatte nicht den Geringsten aus der Jungmünchener Schule für sich geworben: Albert Schlopsnies, einen jungen Ostpreußen, der Franz Stuck zum Lehrer gehabt hatte. Es mag nicht aus der Schule geplaudert sein, wenn man den Werdegang des jungen Malers erzählt. Er stak im Laden eines kaufmännischen Onkels tief in Ostpreußen, war sehr unglücklich, bekritzelte jedes Stück Papier mit Zeichnungen und bat um eine Künstlerzukunft. Vergeblich. Da nahm er sein Rad und fuhr von Tilsit nach München. Franz Stuck, dem er seine Zeichnungen vorlegte, erfuhr's und nahm den begabten Künstler als Schüler an. Bei der ausgesprochenen kunstgewerblichen zweiten Seele des Meisters mußte der Schüler wohl Freude an kunstgewerblichen Formen finden. Und in Giengen, da er sich vor große Experimente gestellt sah, mußte wohl das in München wachgerufene Talent seine Früchte bringen. Wer den „Schwalangscher", wie sich der Münchner

Chevauxleger nennt, den Dienstmann, die Holländer und Bauern der Steiff'schen Fabrik kennt, der weiß um heiteres Künstlerschaffen Bescheid. Und dann der Zirkus. Eine bunte Masse von lustigen Figuren wandert in die Manege der kindlichen Spielzeugbewunderer ein; die Clowns, die Musikanten, die Jongleure, die Diener, Chinesen und Singhalesen und das liebe Publikum vereinigen sich mit der ungeheuren Zahl der zähmbaren, wohl dressierten Steiff'schen Tiere.

Die großen Spielwarenhandlungen und die großen Warenhäuser haben diesen Zirkus und ähnliche umfangreiche Gruppen der Giengener Puppenwelt längst als Clou der Schaufensterdekoration verwertet. Sie haben den Weihnachtsmann zur Sammelwut verführt. Er legt die wundervollen Siebensachen alljährlich partieweise unter den Weihnachtsbaum und läßt für das nächste Christkind den Zuwachs erhoffen. Immer mehr und mehr. Und immer Neues und Schönes. Und der Erfindereifer gab köstliche Zutaten zu den Puppen, indem er ihre ganze natürliche

⑥ „Die Sensationen des Weihnachtsmannes". Entwurf von Alb. Schlopsnies.

copied the whole natural environment, barrack squares and rooms, drill ground for the soldiers, school for children and schoolmaster, taverns for the musicians, arena for the circus and kitchen for the female cook. A little city with little people. When a large German company unpacked the shipping crates full of the Steiff dolls and their backgrounds and put them in the show window, it was awarded a victory in the decoration competition.

The versatility of the company is shown not only in the diversity of the doll playthings, but also in the technical and professional feasibility to give life to the dolls and animals, considering a child's demands, and the solid materials used for the production which are resistant to the destructive fury of our children. This presented many riddles for the inventor's workshop.

And last, but not least, in a tremendous addition to the factory, thousands of kites were produced yearly. The famous triumphant Roloplan kites of the Steiff company, whose carrying capacity made even flight by man possible due to their exceptional stability and steadfast suspension, contributed to the fact that this beautiful and interesting sport finds attention in Germany today which it rightly deserves.
Georg Queri-Munich.

① „Gala-Abend bei Sarrasani". Entwurf von Albert Schlopsnies.

②

Nebenstehende Photographie ist mit einem gewöhnlichen Momentapparat aus einer Höhe von 200 m mittels Roloplandrachen Nr. 180/2 gemacht.

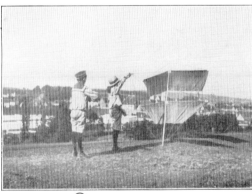

④ Roloplandrachen-Sport.

③ Ikarosflügel.

Umgebung kopierte, Kasernenhof und -stube, den Exerzierplatz zu den Soldaten, die Schule zu Kindern und Schulmeister, die Schenke zu den Dorfmusikanten, die Arena zum Zirkus, die Küche zur Köchin. Eine kleine Stadt mit kleinen Leuten. Und als eine große deutsche Firma den Steiff'schen Apparat von Puppen und Umgebung kurzerhand aus der Versandkiste in das Schaufenster stellte, erhielt sie in einer Dekorationskonkurrenz den Sieg zuerteilt.

Die Vielseitigkeit des Hauses zeigt sich nicht allein in der Verschiedenheit der Puppenspielzeuge. Die technischen Betriebsmöglichkeiten, die Puppen und Tieren Leben geben, wie es das Kind fordert, und die massiven Herstellungsstoffe, vor denen die Zerstörungswut unserer Kleinen wirkungslos bleibt, gaben auch manche Rätsel für die Erfinderwerkstatt. Und — last not least — in einem gewaltigen Anbau der Fabrik werden jährlich Tausende von Drachen hergestellt. Die berühmten sieghaften Roloplan-Drachen der Firma Steiff, die in ihrer Tragkraft selbst den Menschenflug ermöglichen, sind durch ihre außerordentliche Stabilität und Schwebebeständigkeit mit daran schuld, daß der schöne und interessante Sport nun auch in Deutschland die Aufmerksamkeit findet, die ihm gebührt.   Georg Queri-München.

15

PART THREE
1913

All of these ads are from the German publication *Illustrirte Zeitung*.

STEIFF: BUTTON IN EAR

Toy factory Margarete Steiff, G.m.b.H., Giengen. a. Brenz (Württemberg).
Founder and manufacturer of the world famous "teddy bears."
Trademark: Button in Ear
No shipment to private buyers.
Catalog #20-free.

Camel, felt and plush, on strong wooden wheels 43cm (17in) tall, M. 11.50
Camel rider 50cm (20in) tall, M. 7.25
Plush teddy bear, in various colors 25cm (10in) tall, M. 2.10
Plush Record-Peter on wheels, various colors 25cm (10in) tall, M. 4.75

Clown *Noso* 43cm (17in) tall, M. 6.25

Clown *Coloro* 43cm (17in) tall, M. 7.75

Golliwog 28cm (11in) tall, M. 2.40

Steiff toys are available everywhere.
Caesar in shiny plush
The prices apply only in Germany.
22cm (9in) tall, M. 3.75

17

1914

STEIFF: BUTTON IN EAR

Trademark of the clothes, toy animals and dolls. Available everywhere. No direct shipment to private party. Catalog #20 free. Steiff advertising tokens can be obtained in all toy stores. Where not obtainable, party can request it free through the toy factory Margarete Steiff, G.m.b.H., Geingen-Brenz (Württemberg).

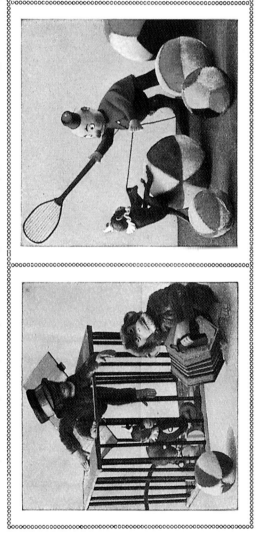

STEIFF · KNOPF IM OHR

Schutzmarke der weltberühmten Stoff-Spieltiere und -Puppen. Ueberall zu haben. Kein direkter Versand an Private. Katalog No. 20 gratis. Steiff-Reklame-Marken sind in jeder Spielwarenhandlung erhältlich, wo nicht, Versand direkt und gratis durch die **Spielwarenfabrik Margarete Steiff, G. m. b. H., Giengen-Brenz** (Württemberg).

1912

STEIFF: BUTTON IN EAR

Cloth animals and dolls in first-class quality. Each piece carries a trademark "Button in Ear." Grand Prix St. Louis 1904 and Brussels 1910.
No direct shipment to private party.
Can be obtained everywhere at German store prices.
Margarete Steiff, G.b.m.H., Giengen-Brenz. Founder and manufacturer of the world famous "teddy bear."
Catalog #20 free and post-paid.

Deer	1399	M.100.	Stork	1143	M.6.00
Giraffe	1180	M.16.50	Lion	1335/2	M.12.0
Polar bear	1343/2	M.21.00	St. Bernard	1528/0	M.3.60
Elephant	1243/2	M.15.60	Swan	2122	M.4.20
Zebra	1243	M.10.80	Duck	2122	M.3.60
Rabbit	2317	M.4.20	Dachauer	129	M.3.30
Dog-Spitz	3322	M.2.70	Clown	323	M.3.60
Teddy bear	5320	M.2.80	Plush ball	310/4E	M.1.05
Elfin woman	35	M.3.30	Plush ball	317/7E	M.2.70
Mini snake	22	M.6.50	Plush ball	325/10E	M.5.70

STEIFF · KNOPF IM OHR

Stofftiere und Puppen in erstklassiger Ausführung. — Jedes Stück trägt als Schutzmarke einen „Knopf im Ohr". — Grand Prix St. Louis 1904 und Brüssel 1910. — Kein direkter Versand an Private.

Überall erhältlich zu deutschen Ladenpreisen. **Margarete Steiff, G.m.b.H., Giengen-Brenz.** Erfinder und Fabrikanten des weltberühmten „Teddy-Bären".

Katalog Nr. 20 gratis und franko.

	cm				cm				cm	
Hirsch	1399	· · · M. 100.—	Storch	1143	: M. 6.—	Hase	2317	· · M. 4.20	Dachauer	129	· · · M. 3.30
Giraffe	1180	· · · M. 16.50	Löwe	1335/2	: M. 12.—	Spitzer	3322	: M. 2.70	Clown	323	· · · M. 3.60
Eisbär	1343/2	· · M. 21.—	Bernhardiner	1528.0	: M. 3.60	Teddy Bär	5320	: M. 2.80	Plüschball	310/4 E.	M. 1.05
Elefant	1243/2	· · M. 15.60	Schwan	2122	: M. 4.20	Alb-Bauer	35	: M. 3.30	Plüschball	317/7 E.	M. 2.70
Zebra	1243.	· · M. 10.80	Ente	2122	: M. 3.60	Zwerg Snak	22	: M. 6.50	Plüschball	325/10 E.	M. 5.70

21

1913

Felt rabbit #3104, 4cm (2in) tall, M.0.30
Plush rabbit #2310, 12cm (5in) tall, M.1.75
Paul #35, 35cm (14in) tall, M.6.00
Plush rabbit #2312, 12cm (5in) tall, M.2.25
Plush ball #308/3E, 8cm (3in) tall, M.0.70
Hilde #35, 35cm (14in) tall, M.6.75
Felt rabbit #3104. 4cm (2in) tall, M.0.30
Plush rabbit #5322, 22cm (9in) tall, M.1.70
Wool rabbit #3508, 8cm (3in) tall, M.0.70
Plush rabbit #2312, 12cm (5in) tall, M.2.25
Velvet rabbit #3404, 4cm (2in) tall, M.0.40
Felt rabbit #3104, 4cm (2in) tall, M.0.30
Plush rabbit #2308, 8cm (3in) tall, M.1.40

Above prices applicable only in Germany. Steiff animals and dolls can be obtained everywhere. Each item carries the trademark "Button in Ear." Toy factory Margarete Steiff, G.b.m.H., founder and manufacturer of the world-famous "teddy bear," Giengen-Brenz (Württemberg). Grand Prix St. Louis 1904 and Brussels 1910. No direct shipment to private party. Catalog #20 free.

STEIFF · KNOPF IM OHR

Filz-Hase   Plüsch-Hase   Paul Nr. 35.   Plüsch-Hase Nr. 2312.   Hilde Nr. 35.   Plüsch-Hase Woll-Hase Nr. 3508.   Sam t-Hase   Filz-Hase   Plüsch-Hase
Nr. 3104.   Nr. 2310.   (35 cm gross).   (12 cm gross). Mk. 2.25.   (35 cm gross). Mk. 6.75.   Nr. 5322.   (8 cm gross). Mk. —.70.   Nr. 3404.   Nr. 3104.   Nr. 2308.
(4 cm gross).   (12 cm gross).   Mk. 6.—.   Plüsch-Ball Nr. 3803/3E.   Filz - Hase Nr. 3104.   (22 cm gross). Plüsch-Hase Nr. 2312. (4 cm gross).   (4 cm gross).   (8 cm gross).
Mk. —.30.   Mk. 1.75.   (8 cm gross). Mk. —.70.   (4 cm gross). Mk. —.30. Mk. 1.70.   (12 cm gross). Mk. 2.25.   Mk. —.40.   Mk. —.30.   Mk. 1.40.

Obige Preise sind nur in Deutschland gültig. — Steiff-Tiere und Puppen sind überall zu haben. — Jedes Stück trägt als Schutzmarke einen „KNOPF IM OHR".
Spielwarenfabrik Margarete Steiff, G. m. b. H., Erfinder und Fabrikanten des weltberühmten „Teddy-Bären", **Giengen-Brenz (Württemberg).**
Grand Prix St Louis 1904 und Brüssel 1910. — Kein direkter Versand an Private. — Katalog Nr. 20 gratis.

PART FOUR
1913

Back row:

Giraffe	#1260/8, 260cm (102in) tall,	M.165.00
Camel	#13160/2/8, 160cm (63in) tall,	M.315.00
Rider	100cm (39in) tall,	M.48.00
Elephant	#1180/2, 80cm (31in) tall,	M.57.00
St. Bernard	#1380/2, 80cm (31in) tall,	M.65.50
Bear	# 1260/2, 60cm (24in) tall,	M.27.00
Horse	#1370/8, 70cm (28in) tall,	M.49.50
Camel	#1160, 60cm (24in) tall,	M.24.00
Lamb	#1560/2, 60cm (24in) tall,	M.27.00

Front Row:

Bear	#1380/2/8, 60cm (24in) tall,	M.69.50
Horse	#1390/8, 90cm (35in) tall,	M.78.00
Lion	#1360/2, 60cm (24in) tall,	M.43.00
Elephant	#1260/2, 50cm (20in) tall,	M.36.00
Polar bear	#1350/2, 50cm (20in) tall,	M.25.80

The mentioned prices are applicable only in Germany. For abroad raise price for freight and custom duty. Margarete Steiff, G.m.b.H., Giengen-Brenz (Württemberg).

Founder and manufacturer of the world famous "teddy bear." Cloth soft-stuffed toys and animals. Unsurpassed in quality and artistic interpretation. Each item carries the "Button in Ear" trademark. Please look for it when you buy. Grand Prix St. Louis 1904 and Brussels 1910. Steiff animals and dolls available everywhere. Catalog #20 free.

STEIFF KNOPF IM OHR

Hintere
Reihe:

Kamel Nr. 13160/2/8. (160 cm gross). Mark 315.—	Elefant Nr. 1180/2. (80 cm gross). Mark 57.—	Bernhardiner Nr. 1380/2. (80 cm gross). Mark 65.50.	Bär Nr. 1260/2. (60 cm gross). Mark 27.—
		Pferd Nr. 1370.8. (70 cm gross). Mark 49.50.	Kamel Nr. 1160. (60 cm gross). Mark 24.—
			Lamm Nr. 1560/2. (60 cm gross). Mark 27.—

Vordere
Reihe:

Bär Nr. 1380/2.8. (60 cm gross). Mark 69.50.	Pferd Nr. 1390/8. (90 cm gross). Mark 78.—	Löwe Nr. 1360/2. (60 cm gross). Mark 43.—	Elefant Nr. 1260/2. (60 cm gross). Mark 36.—	Gaucho (100 cm gross). Mark 48.—	Polar-Bär Nr. 1350/2. (50 cm gross). Mark 25.80.	Giraffe Nr. 11260/8. (260 cm gross). Mark 165.—

Die angeführten Preise sind nur in Deutschland gültig.
Für's Ausland erhöhen sich jsolche durch Fracht und Zoll.

Margarete Steiff, G. m. b. H., Giengen-Brenz (Württemberg).

Erfinder und Fabrikanten des weltberühmten „Teddy"-Bären. Fabrik weichgestopfter Spiel-Tiere und -Puppen. Unerreicht in Qualität und künstlerischer Ausführung. Jedes Stück trägt einen „KNOPF IM OHR" als Schutzmarke. Achten Sie bitte beim Einkauf darauf. Grand Prix St. Louis 1904 und Brüssel 1910. Steiff-Tiere und Puppen sind überall zu haben. Katalog Nr. 20 gratis.

1913

Toy factory Margarete Steiff, G.m.b.H., Giengen a. Brenz (Württemberg), founder and manufacturer of the world-famous "teddy bear." Available everywhere. Trademark: Button in Ear. Catalog # 20 free. No direct shipment to private party.

Shiny plush poodle with pull voice #1343.2, 43cm (17in) tall, M.16.50

Doll *Loni*, felt, genuinely dressed #35, 35cm (14in) tall, M.6.25

Duck, velvet painted #2417, 17cm (7in) tall, M.2.30

Plush ball #320/8E, 20cm (8in) tall, M.3.50

Dachauer #35, 35cm (14in) tall, M.3.00

Wool plush elephant #1522.0, 22cm (9in) tall, M.3.00

Doll *Hilde*, felt, adorably dressed #35, 35cm (14in) tall, M.6.75

Teddy bear, shiny plush #5328.2, 40cm (16in) tall, M.6.75

Infantry soldier, 50cm (20in) tall, M.8.50

Velvet mouse #2404, 4cm (2in) tall, M.0.40

Fox terrier, shiny plush #3322, 22cm (9in) tall, M.2.70

1914

Chirping ducks, on eccentric wooden wheels,
white plush mohair, 190gm (7oz) #6314.2ex,
14cm (6in) tall, retail price M.3.00
Swan, white plush mohair, 420gm (15oz) #5335,
24cm (9in) tall, retail price M.6.50

Steiff original toys available in all better toy stores. Catalog #20 free on request.

Trademark of the world famous Steiff toys. Available in all better toy stores. Steiff advertisement through Margarete Steiff, G.m.b.H., Giengen-Brenz (Württemberg). Catalog #20 free.

STEIFF KNOPF IM OHR

Schutzmarke der weltberühmten Steiff-Spielwaren · In jedem besseren Spielwarengeschäft zu haben (Steiff-Reklame-Marken gratis durch **Margarete Steiff, G. m. b. H., Giengen-Brenz** (Württemberg) · Katalog Nr 20 gratis

Artistic cloth animals from the toy factory. Margarete Steiff, G.m.b.H. Giengen-Brenz (Württemberg). Grand Prix St. Louis 1904, Brussels 1910. Catalog #20 free.

STEIFF IM OHR

Künstler-Stofftiere und Puppen aus der Spielwarenfabrik Margarete Steiff, G. m. b. H., Giengen a. Brenz (Württemberg). Grands Prix St. Louis 1904. Brüssel 1910. Katalog No. 20 gratis.

33

1911

Not to be missing on your Christmas table: the world-famous animals and dolls with "Button in Ear" from the toy factory of Margarete Steiff, G.m.b.H., Giengen-Brenz, Grand Prix St. Louis 1904 and Brussels 1910. Available everywhere. No direct shipment to private buyer. Catalog #20 free.

Back row:
    Olaf 43cm (17in) tall, M.8.00
    Plush camel #1350, 50cm (20in) tall, M.20.75
    Plush rabbit, jointed #5328, 28cm (11in) tall, M.2.40
    Plush ox #1235, 35cm (14in) tall, M.8.40
    Plush rabbit #1217, 17cm (7in) tall, M.2.80
    Lamb #1517, 17cm (7in) tall, M.1.70
    Lamb #1522, 22cm (9in) tall, M.2.70
    Lamb #6522, 22cm (9in) tall, M.2.80

Front row:
    Clown 100cm (39in) tall, M.21.40
    Plush horse with steering #1370.8, 70cm (28in) tall, M.57.00
    Plush elephant with voice #1260.2, 60cm (24in) tall, M.36.00

Obere Reihe: Olaf 43 cm   Plüsch-Kamel Nr. 1350   Plüsch-Ochse Nr. 1343,2   Plüsch-Esel Nr. 1235   Lamm Nr. 1517 (17 cm hoch) Mk. 1.70
               Mk. 8.—   (50 cm hoch) Mk. 20.75   (43 cm hoch, mit Stimme)   (35 cm hoch) Mk. 8.40   Lamm Nr. 1522 (22 cm hoch) Mk. 2.70
Untere Reihe   Clown 100 cm   Plüsch-Pferd Nr. 1370,8   Mk. 15.60   Plüsch-Hase Nr. 1217   Lamm Nr. 6522 (22 cm hoch) Mk. 2.80
               Mk. 21.40   (70 cm hoch) m. Lenkung Mk. 57.—   Plüsch-Hase Nr. 5328   (17 cm hoch) Mk. 2.80
                                                               gegliedert (28 cm hoch)
                                  Plüsch-Elefant Nr. 1260,2   Mk. 2.40
                                  (60 cm hoch) m. Stimme Mk. 36.—

Rabbit, sitting, white plush mohair, #2317, 17cm (7in) tall, 240gm (8oz). Retail price M.3.00
Rabbit, standing, white plush mohair, #4322, 22cm (9in) tall, 100gm (4oz). Retail price M.1.70
Squealing pig, standing, rose plush mohair, #1317.0.1, 120 gm (4oz), 17cm (7in) tall. Retail price M.2.60
Teddy bear, jointed, white plush mohair, #5320, sits 20cm (8in) tall, 210gm (7oz). Retail price M.2.80
Tufted bear, standing, white plush mohair, #1328.0.1, with press bellows voice, 28cm (11in) tall, 500gm (17oz). Retail price M.8.75

Margarete Steiff, G.m.b.H., Giengen-Brenz (Württemberg). Founder and manufacturer of the world-famous "teddy bear." Steiff toys are available everywhere. Catalog #20 free to interested parties.

STEIFF KNOPF IM OHR
SPIELWAREN

Hase, liegend, aus weiss Mohair-Plüsch Nr 2317, 17 cm hoch, 240 gr schwer Detailpreis: M 3.—

Obige Preise gelten nur für Deutschland

Oben: **Hase,** aufwartend, weiss Mohair-Plüsch, Nr 4322 22 cm hoch, 10C gr schwer, Detailpreis: M 1.70
Unten: **Quietsch-Schwein,** steh., aus rosa Mohair-Plüsch Nr 1317,0.1,120 gr schwer,17 cm hoch, Detailpreis: M2.60

Teddy-Bär, gegliedert, aus weiss Mohair-Plüsch, Nr 5320 Sitzhöhe 20 cm, 210 gr schwer Detailpreis: M 2.80

Margarete Steiff, G.m.b.H., Giengen-Brenz (Württemberg)
Erfinder und Fabrikanten des weltberühmten Teddy-Bären

Zottelbär, stehend, aus weiss Mohair-Plüsch, Nr 1328,0.1 mit Druckbalg-stimme, 28 cm hoch, 500 gr schwer Detailpreis: M 8.75

Steiff-Spielwaren sind überall zu haben Katalog Nr 20 an Interessenten gratis

37

1930

The trademark of the world-famous natural-looking cloth animals from Margarete Steiff. The silent artistic play-friends of children whose fantasies always lead to new ideas. They may also enchant a lady who has a collection of Steiff animals. Available everywhere. Brochure L free.

STEIFF KNOPF IM OHR

Elefant aus Filz mit reich verzierter Schabracke, 60 cm hoch, 75 cm lang, Gewicht 8 kg. — Tragkraft bis 20 Ctr; mit stark tönender Zugstimme Nr 1160,2 Detailpreis für Deutschland M 28.—

Schimpanse aus braunem Glanzplüsch, gegliedert, 17 cm hoch, sitzend, Nr 9/5317 M 3.—

In allen Spielwarenhandlungen zu haben — Kein direkter Versand an Private — **Margarete Steiff** G. m. b. H. Spielwarenfabrik **Giengen-**Brenz Württ. Katalog Nr 20 gratis.

1914

Felt elephant with richly decorated saddle cloth, 60cm (24in) tall, 75cm (30in) long, weighs 8kg (18lb), transverse strength up to 20 Ctr., with loud-sounding pull noise, #1160.2, retail price in Germany M.28.00
Chimpanzee, brown shiny plush, jointed, sitting, 17cm (7in) tall, #9/5317 M.3.0
Available in all toy stores. No direct shipment to private parties.
Margarete Steiff, G.m.b.H., Toy factory Giengen-Brenz (Württemberg). Catalog #20 free.

PART FIVE
1913

"Teddy bear" is an original creation and wholesale item of the toy factory Margarete Steiff, Giengen-Brenz (Württemberg).

Steiff "teddy bear," the overwhelming darling of all children in the world, carries the trademark "Button in Ear" and is available everywhere. Reject copies. Ask specifically for "Steiff originals." Highest awards: Grand Prix St. Louis 1904 and Brussels 1910. Illustrated price lists #20 free and postpaid. Prices applicable only in Germany.

5350.2 with growl voice 70cm (28in) M.21.50
5343.2 with growl voice 60cm (24in) M.16.00
5335.2 with growl voice 50cm (20in) M.11.25
5332.2 with growl voice 46cm (18in) M.8.70
5328.2 with growl voice 40cm (16in) M.6.75

5325.2 with growl voice 35cm (14in) M.5.20
5322.2 with growl voice 32cm (13in) M.4.20
5322 with squeaky voice 32cm (13in) M.3.60
5317 with squeaky voice 25cm (10in) M.2.10
5315 with squeaky voice 22cm (9in) M.1.70

STEIFF · KNOPF IM OHR

Margarete Steiff, G.m.b.H., Spielwarenfabrik in Giengen-Brenz (Württbg.)
Erfinder und Fabrikanten des weltberühmten „Teddy-Bären".
Jedes Stück trägt als Schutzmarke einen „Knopf im Ohr": Grand Prix St. Louis 1904 u. Brüssel 1910.

„Rekord-Teddy-Bären" aus hellbraunem Glanzplüsch auf Selbstfahrer mit automatischer Stimme. Höhe 25 cm. Länge 23 cm. Gewicht 540 gramm. Detailpreis (nur in Deutschland gültig) Mk. 4.— per Stück in elegantem Karton. Kein direkter Versand an Private. Katalog No. 20 gratis. In allen Spielwarenhandlungen zu haben.

1913

Margarete Steiff, G.m.b.H., Toy factory is Giengen-Brenz (Württemberg).
Founder and manufacturer of the world-famous "teddy bear." Each item carries the trademark "Button in Ear."
Grand Prix St. Louis 1904 and Brussels 1910.

Record Teddy Bears, light brown shiny plush with automatic voices. 25cm (10in) tall, 23cm (9in) long, 540gm (19oz). Retail price (valid only in Germany) M.4.00. No direct sale to private party. Catalog #20 free. Each item in an elegant box. Available in all toy stores.

1913

Record Peter #17; everywhere for M.5.50
Retail catalog sent out by Margarete Steiff, Giengen-
Brenz. #20.

1925

The good toy.
Available everywhere. Brochure L and picture catalog
free.
Margarete Steiff, G.m.b.H., Toy factory, Giengen a.
Brenz 7 (Württemberg).

STEIFF TRETOMOBIL

Das elegante, fahrsichere Kinderauto.

Starke Konstruktion, Antrieb durch rahmenartige Tretpendel mit gekugelter Lagerung und günstiger Übersetzung, daher leichte, geräuschlose Fortbewegung selbst an Steigungen. Große, auswechselbare Metallscheibenräder mit Vollgummireifen. Steuerung leicht und sicher, gute Abrollbremse, Sitz gepolstert, Tretlänge verstellbar für 4–10 Jahre. Hupe, Richtungszeiger, Pufferstangen, Reserverad, Soziussitz. Elegante, spiegelglatte Lackierung. Tragkraft bis zu vier Kinder.

Zu haben in Spielwarengeschäften. Farbiger Spezialprospekt LF kostenfrei.

Margarete Steiff G. m. b. H., Giengen a. Brenz 7 (Württ.).

1925

Steiff Tretomobil
The elegant safe-to-drive car for children.

Sturdy construction. Powered through framelike tread pedal with ball bearing and favorable gear ratio; therefore, easy quiet movement even on inclines. Large, interchangeable metal disc wheels with solid rubber tires. Easy steering and safe, good brakes, upholstered seat. Pedals adjustable for four to ten- year-olds. Motor horn, direction indicator, bumper, spare wheel, passenger seat. Elegant, mirror-like lacquer. Can carry up to four children. Available in toy stores. Free LF special color brochure.
Margarete Steiff G.m.b.H. Giengen a. Brenz 7 (Württemberg).

Sonnige Kindheit

bereiten Sie Ihrem Liebling
durch eine Sammlung der formenschönen Spieltiere **Marke**

STEIFF · Knopf im Ohr

Wie beglückt sind Kinder, wenn die kleinen Händchen das seiden=
weiche Plüschfell streicheln, eine Vielzahl von Bewegungen und Stellungen
formen und ihre Phantasie ihnen Leben einhaucht. Steiff=Spieltiere
sind weltberühmt durch Schönheit, Güte und Preiswürdigkeit.

Zu haben in Spielwarengeschäften. Prospekt L auf Wunsch.

Margarete Steiff G. m. b. H., Giengen a. Brenz 7 (Württ.).

1929

Sunny Childhood for your darling with a collection of
beautifully shaped toy animals with the trademark Steiff
Button in Ear.

How happy children are when their little hands stroke the
soft plush, create many movements and poses and see
them as being alive in their fantasies. Steiff toy animals are
world-famous for their beauty, excellent materials and
good value. Available in toy stores. Brochure L on request.
Margarete Steiff, G.m.b.H., Giengen a. Brenz 7 (Württemberg).

1914

"Record teddy bears" #25, light brown shiny plush. Stable riding with strong wooden wheels. No breakable parts. On a pull string. Automatic voice. 25cm (10in) tall, 23cm (9in) long, 540gm (19oz). Retail price in Germany M.4.00, in Austria K.6. Available everywhere. No direct sale to private party. Trademark "Button in Ear." Catalog #20 free. Toy factory Margarete Steiff, G.m.b.H., Giengen-Brenz (Württemberg).

Founder and manufacturer of the world-famous "teddy bear." Grand Prix St. Louis 1904 and Brussels 1910. International trade exhibition, Leipzig 1913: State award.

1929

There is joy!
Reach for the beautiful animal products of Margarete
Steiff, depicting the world-famous quality and beauty.
Reasonably priced and ready to make all children happy.
Therefore, for Easter:
Steiff: Button in Ear
Available everywhere. Color brochures free.
Margarete Steiff, G.m.b.H., Giengen a. Brenz 7 (Würt-
temberg).

Beautiful toy animals full of expression. World famous
quality and perfection. Available everywhere. Brochure L
free.

Ganz bei der Sache

im Spiel mit

STEIFF-
Kindersport-Fahrzeugen

Elegante Form, leichtester Lauf auf gekugelten Lagern (pat.), hervorragende Lenkfähigkeit und Fahrsicherheit, große Tragkraft, preiswerte Qualitätsarbeit.
Zu haben in guten Spielwaren-Geschäften. Ausführlicher Fahrzeugprospekt und Nachweis kostenfrei.

Margarete Steiff G. m. b. H., Giengen a. Brenz 7 (Württ.)

Totally engrossed when playing with Steiff Children's Sports Car
Elegant style, smooth ride on ball bearing wheels (pat.), outstanding steering and great stability. Excellent value and quality work.
Available in good stores. Detailed brochure and information free of charge.
Margarete Steiff, G.m.b.H., Giengen a. Brenz 7 (Württemberg).

PART SIX

STEIFF: BUTTON IN EAR

The Leading Mark of Quality

Ask for it in all toy stores. Brochure L and picture pamphlet free.
Margarete Steiff B.m.b.H., toy factory, Giengen a. Brenz 7 (Württemberg).

Autos gibt es ohne Zahl
doch nur eins
aus „Bärkopf-Stahl"

Gesunde Bewegung ist eine Hauptforderung aller Zeiten. Die bewährten Steiff-Kindersport-Fahrzeuge gewährleisten nicht nur gesundes Spielen, sondern auch hohe Sicherheit und Dauerhaftigkeit und dadurch lange Freude. Sie bieten bei großer Preiswürdigkeit elegante Form, leichtesten Lauf auf gekugelten Lagern (pat.), hervorragende Lenkfähigkeit und Fahrsicherheit, große Tragkraft, Sitzverstellung und Türe.

Achten Sie auf die Bärkopf-Marke.

Steiff-Autos 28.— bis 89.— RM.
Steiff-Roller 3.90 bis 9.50 RM.

Überall zu haben.
Ausführlicher Prospekt LF und Nachweis kostenfrei.

Margarete Steiff G. m. b. H., Giengen a. Brenz 7 (Württ.).

There are many cars, but only one from "Bearkopf-Stahl."
Sound movement is in demand at all times. The trustworthy Steiff children's sports cars provide not only healthy play, but also safety and durability, giving long-lasting pleasure. They are reasonably priced, give an elegant smooth ride on ball bearings (pat.), exceptional steering and safety, great carrying capacity, adjustable seat and doors.
Look for the "Bear Head" trademark.

Available everywhere. Detailed brochure LF and information free.
Margarete Steiff, G.m.b.H., Giengen a. Brenz 7 (Württemberg).

Steiff Button in Ear.
The leading mark of quality.

STEIFF
KNOPF IM OHR

Die erstaunliche Haltbarkeit und Unverwüstlichkeit der Steiff-Stofftiere und Puppen ist bekannt; daher verlangen Kenner immer wieder Steiff-Spielzeug mit der Marke „Knopf im Ohr". Überall zu haben. Grand Prix St. Louis 1904 und Brüssel 1910.

Margarete Steiff, G.m.b.H, Spielwarenfabrik, **Giengen** a. Brenz. Erfinder und Fabrikanten des weltberühmten „Teddy-Bären".

Kein direkter Versand an Private. Katalog Nr. 20 gratis.

The surprising durability and indestructibility of the Steiff cloth animals and dolls is well-known; that is why an expert always demands Steiff toys with the trademark "Button in Ear." Available everywhere. Grand Prix St. Louis 1904 and Brussels 1910. Margarete Steiff, G.m.b.H., toy factory, Giengen a. Brenz. Founder and manufacturer of the world-famous "teddy bear." No direct shipment to private party. Catalog #20 free.

The breakable porcelain dolls with their molded features are becoming more and more the dolls of the "new trend." The Steiff caricatures are the pioneers of the doll reform, are made completely from cloth, authentically dressed and are gradually taking their lead in the doll world because of their durability and unbreakability. Their humorous style is met everywhere with enthusiastic recognition. The highest distinction Grand Prix St. Louis 1904 and Brussels 1910. Each "Original Steiff Doll" carries the trademark "Button in Ear" with the name of the maker. Margarete Steiff, toy factory, Giengen a. Brenz. No shipment to private party. Catalog #20 free.

Marine Lieutenant 60 TD, 60cm (24in) tall, M.9.75
Captain 50 TD, 50cm (20in) tall, M.18.75
Sailor 50 TD, 50cm (20in) tall, M.9.00
These prices are valid only in Germany.

Steiff caricature dolls are unbreakable and mobile. The joints can be naturally positioned and do not creak when moved. The material on the arms and legs is reinforced. The Steiff caricature dolls are not hard or heavy; they will not hurt a child; they also have fabrics that will not discolor. Steiff caricature dolls are not filled with sawdust, only with pure wood shavings. The body and limbs cannot spill their contents and maintain their plastic-like form. The dresses of the Steiff caricature dolls are genuine in every detail. Each item carries a "Button in Ear" as a trademark. Steiff caricature dolls come in sizes from 22cm (9in) to 100cm (39in) and are carried in all better toy stores. Reject copies. Ask specifically for "Original Steiff." Catalog #20 with pictures of the toy animals and dolls is free upon request. Margarete Steiff, toy factory, Giengen-Brenz. Founder and manufacturer of the world-famous "teddy bear." Grand Prix: World Exhibition St. Louis 1904 and Brussels 1910.

Infantry Lieutenant 60cm (24in), M.7.20
Fox terrier 1414.0, M.1.30
Sentry-box 62cm (24in), M.6.75
Infantry sentry with rifle 50cm (20in), M.11.70
Karoline 50cm (20in), M.18.00
These prices are valid in Germany only.

Why do experts, when buying toys, always demand Steiff original animals and dolls with the "Button in Ear?" Because they know that they are getting the most beautiful and lasting toys for the least price. A toy that small children can be trusted with, without worry that it will be damaged, because the Steiff toy animals and dolls are unbreakable and outlive all other toys. The highest distinction: Grand Prix St. Louis 1904 and Brussels 1910. Margarete Steiff, G.m.b.H., toy factory, Giengen a. Brenz. Founder and manufacturer of the world-famous "teddy bear." No shipment to private party. Catalog #20 free. The following prices are valid in Germany only.

Farmer 50cm (20in) tall, M.14.25
Ox with pull voice #1343,2, 43cm (17in) tall, M.15.60
Ox with pull voice #1335,2, 35cm (14in) tall, M.10.50

Nr. 3595. 23. Mai 1912. Illustrirte Zeitung.

STEIFF
KNOPF IM OHR

Die Vorzüge der Steiff Stoff-Tiere und Puppen liegen in ihrer Unzerbrechlichkeit und Strapazierfähigkeit. Wenn anderes Spielzeug längst zerbrochen und seinen Reiz verloren hat, greift das Kind wieder zur bewährten Marke „Knopf im Ohr"; denn Steiff Tiere und Puppen überdauern alle anderen Spielsachen. Grand Prix St. Louis 1904 und Brüssel 1910. — Überall erhältlich.

**Margarete Steiff, G. m. b. H.,
Spielwaren - Fabrik, Giengen a. Brenz.**
Erfinder und Fabrikanten des weltberühmten „Teddy - Bären".

Kein direkter Versand an Private.   Katalog Nr. 20 gratis.

1912

The superiority of the Steiff cloth animals and toys lies in their stability and durability. Long after other toys are broken or have lost their appeal, a child will reach for the trademark "Button in Ear," because Steiff animals and toys outlive all other toys. Grand Prix St. Louis 1904 and Brussels 1910. Available everywhere. Margarete Steiff, G.m.b.H., toy factory, Giengen a. Brenz. Founder and manufacturer of the world-famous "teddy bear." No direct shipment to private party. Catalog #20 free.

Ulan mit Pferd 1142 a feldmäßige Ausrüstung (Pferd mit Räder) Gesamthöhe 55 cm; Detailpreis in Deutschland zus. M 28.50 das Stück. — Franzos 35T (35 cm groß) M 5.20 das Stück.

Animals and dolls, soft stuffed, are known for their durability and original natural expression. Each item carries the trademark "Button in Ear." Available everywhere. Toy factory of Margarete Steiff, G.m.b.H., Giengen-Brenz (Württemburg). Catalog with 1800 listings #20 free.

Lancer with horse #1142a moderate battlefield equipment (horse with rider), total height 55cm (22in); retail price in Germany is M.28.50 per item. Frenchmen 35T, 35cm (14in) tall, M.5.20 per item.

PART SEVEN

Steiff riding and movable animals possess an astonishing carrying capacity. Beautiful shapes, quality workmanship. The best from the best. Available in all toy stores. Illustrated brochure L free of charge. Margarete Steiff G.m.b.H., first factory of soft-stuffed toys, Giengen a. Brenz 7 (Württemberg).

Elephant made out of felt or short plush with richly decorated saddle cloth and with a vibrant pull-voice, transverse strength, carries up to 1000g (2205lb). 50cm (20in) high, weighs 5kg (11lb).
#1150,2 - felt, retail price M.19.00
#1250,2 - short plush, retail price M.23.50
Above prices applicable only in Germany. Available in all toy stores. Margarete Steiff, G.m.b.H., toy factory Giengen-Brenz (Württemberg) Catalog #20 free.

Children are friends of animals and they want to play with *Teddy, Molly, Bully* or their riding horse. The soft-stuffed Steiff animals with the "Button in Ear" are so right to play with and to love. Beautiful, durable and a good value. An ever welcome gift. Available in toy stores. Color illustrated brochure L free of charge. Margarete Steiff G.m.b.H., Giengen a. Brenz 7 (Württemberg).

Giving is easy when one knows that Steiff animals enthuse the youngsters. Steiff toys with the "Button in Ear" are extraordinarily beautiful, cozy, soft, durable and a good value. The ever popular, elegant present. Available in good toy stores. Color brochure L free of cost. Margarete Steiff G.m.b.H., Giengen a. Brenz 7 (Württemberg).

Steiff--Button in Ear
The good toy. Available everywhere.
Brochure L and picture catalog free.
Margarete Steiff G.m.b.H., Giengen
a. Brenz 7 (Württemberg).

Steiff children's sports cars offer the sports-enthusiastic youngsters the most wonderful pleasure in the open air and can be mastered by even the smallest tots. Steiff "Bear-kopf" scooters and cars are elegant, indestructible and known for a gentle ride. Brochure L232 and information free of charge from Margarete Steiff G.m.b.H., Giengen a. Brenz 7 (Württemberg).

Katzlady	**Katzbaby**	Ob.: **Katze** a. Lammplüsch 17 cm hoch, 70 gr schwer Nr 3517 Detailpreis: M 1.70 Unten: **Katze** aus Samt 8 cm hoch, 40 gr schwer Nr 2408,4 Detailpr.: M –.80	**Gestiefelter Kater** (ohne Instrument) grau-weiß, mit Miau-stimme, 43 cm hoch, 500 gr schwer, Nr 43,2 Detailpreis: M 13.—	**Katze,** weiß Mohairplüsch 17 cm hoch 100 gr schwer Nr 1317,0 De-tailpr.: M 2,10	**Katze** a. Kurz-plüsch, grau be-malt, 17 cm hoch 90 gr schwer Nr 3217 Detail-preis: M 1.70	Oben: **Katze** a. wß. Mohairplüsch 28 cm hoch, 250 gr schwer, Nr 3328 Detailpr.: M 4.25 Unten: **Katze** aus grau-weiß Mohairplüsch mit Miau-Stimme, 22 cm hoch, 260 gr schwer, Nr 5322,2 Detailpr.: M 4.50	**Angora-Katze** aus Mohairplüsch weiß und gefleckt 22 cm hoch, 350 gr schwer, Nr 1322 A Detailpreis: M 4.50
grau-weiß, m. Miau-Stimme 22 cm hoch, 200 gr schwer Nr 22,2 Detailpreis: M 3.75	Nr 22,2 M 3.50						

Cat lady, gray and white, 22cm (9in) tall,
#22,2 retail price M.3.75
Cat baby with meow voice weighs 200gm (7oz),
#22,2 retail price M.3.50
Cat, lamb plush, 17cm (7in) tall, 70gm (2oz),
#3517 retail price M.1.70
Cat, velvet, 8cm (3in) tall, 40gm (1.4oz),
#2408,4 retail price M.0.80
Puss in Boots, without instrument, gray and white,
with meow voice, 43cm (17in) tall, 500gm (17oz),
#43,2 retail price M.13.00
Cat, white plush mohair, 17cm (7in) tall,
100gm (4oz), #1317 retail price M.2.10
Cat, short plush, gray with painted stripes, 17cm (7in) tall,
90gm (3oz), #3217, retail price M.1.70
Cat, white plush mohair, 28cm (11in) tall,
250gm (9oz), #3328, retail price M.4.25
Cat, gray and white plush mohair with meow voice,
22cm (9in) tall, 260gm (9oz), #5322,2 retail price M.4.50
Angora cat, white and speckled plush mohair,
22cm (9in) tall, 350gm (12oz), #1322A retail price M.4.50

Cloth animals and dolls in first-class quality. Durable and indestructible. Each piece carries trademark "Button in Ear."

The Smart Hans

These prices valid only in Germany.
Hans 35cm (14in) tall, M.6.00
#1317 Spitzer, standing with wheels 17cm (7in) tall, M.2.00
#3317 Spitzer, sitting, 17cm (7in) tall, M.1.70
#5317 Spitzer, movable, 17cm (7in) tall, M.2.10
#5317 Goose, movable 17cm (7in) tall, M.2.40
Catalog #20 free; no direct sale to private party. Available only through toy stores. Margarete Steiff, G.m.b.H., Giengen a. Brenz. Founder and manufacturer of the world-famous "teddy bear." Grand Prix St. Louis 1904 and Brussels 1910.

The unbreakable cloth toy animals and dolls with the "Button in Ear" take an extraordinary place in the yearly world export of German toys. Who does not know the cute Steiff original "teddy bear" who took America by storm some years ago and that can be found in the rooms of children the whole world over? But he is not a loner; we see him in merry company of other Steiff animals and dolls who share in his adventures and outlive all their competitors. The "Button in Ear" is their talisman. The workshops of these durable and indestructible toys are situated in large airy buildings with an area of 1800 square meters. Many busy workers reproduce the animals and dolls designed by the artists. Catalog #20, which illustrates the above toys and gives a more detailed description, is free from the toy factory of Margarete Steiff, G.m.b.H., Giengen a. Brenz (Württemberg). It is to be noted that these Steiff animals and dolls received the highest awards at the World's Fair in St. Louis 1904 and Brussels 1910. Steiff toys can be obtained everywhere. No direct shipment to private parties.

Each item carries the trademark "Button in Ear." Steiff original toys are manufactured in the toy factory of Margarete Steiff G.m.b.H., Giengen-Brenz (Württemberg).

STEIFF · KNOPF IM OHR ·

Soldat 50 TD
50 cm groß
Mk. 10.—

Setter 43,2
43 cm;
mit Wam.-St.
Mk. 10.20

Müller-Pferd
60 cm;
mit Geschirr
Mk. 26.25

Moritz
50 cm
Mk. 3.70

Michel
50 cm
Mk. 14.25

(Diese Preise sind
nur in Deutschland
gültig.)

Anton Rutti 43,2
35 cm; 43 cm; mit
Wam.-St.
Mk. 9.60

Hans Larry 43,2
35 cm; 43 cm; mit
Mk. 6.— Wam.-St.
Mk. 8.60

Jonsen Hubertus
43 cm 43 cm
Mk. 7.20 Mk. 8.60

Mar
30 cm
Mk. 2.70

Niba
28 cm
Mk. 5.20

Unter der Unmasse der alljährlich in die Welt gehenden deutschen Spielwaren nehmen seit Jahrzehnten die unzerbrechlichen Stofftiere und -Puppen mit dem "Knopf im Ohr" eine hervorragende Stellung ein. Wer kennt nicht den drolligen Steiff Original "Teddy-Bären", der vor einigen Jahren ganz Amerika im Sturm eroberte und heute in den Kinderstuben der ganzen Welt zu finden ist?! Er führt jedoch da sein Einsiedlerleben, sondern wir sehen ihn in lustiger Gesellschaft anderer Tiere und Puppen, die seine Strapazen ohne jegliches Unbehagen teilen, und alle ihre Nebenbuhler an Langlebigkeit übertreffen. Der "Knopf im Ohr" ist ihr Talisman. Die Werkstätten dieses so dauerhaften und unverwüstlichen Spielzeuges befinden sich in großen luftigen Gebäuden mit einem Gesamtareal von 18000 Quadratmetern und beherbergen viele fleißige Arbeiter und Arbeiterinnen, welche die von Künstlerhand entworfenen Tiere und Puppen herstellen.

Interessenten wird der Katalog Nr. 20, in dem obiges Spielzeug illustriert und näher beschrieben ist, gratis zugestellt von der Spielwarenfabrik Margarete Steiff, G. m. b. H., Giengen a. Brenz, Württemberg. Zu erwähnen bleibt noch, daß die Steiff-Tiere und -Puppen zur Weltausstellung St. Louis 1904 und Brüssel 1910 den Grand Prix (höchste Auszeichnung) erhalten haben. Steiff Spielzeug ist überall erhältlich. Kein direkter Versand an Private.

The decorative plush animals of Margarete Steiff, noble in shape and material, are prized equally in children's playrooms as well as salons. Give pleasure and choose a rattler from 1.90 to 12.50 marks or other animals from the Steiff menagerie. Brochure L 229 is available free from Margarete Steiff G.m.b.H., Geingen a. Brenz 7 (Württemberg).

PART EIGHT

Happy laughter of blessed children enriched by beautiful toys is your greatest Christmas treasure. Choose a Steiff animal with "Button in Ear" to play with or to drive or ride. With the proven Steiff Bearkopf Scooter, children can enjoy a smooth, quiet ride. Steiff toys are beautiful, durable and price-worthy. They enjoy a world-wide reputation.

Steiff Button in Ear: Unsurpassed beauty, durable, price-worthy. The good toy. Available in toy stores. Brochure L free of charge. Margarete Steiff G.m.b.H., Giengen a. Brenz 7 (Württemberg).

Steiff Button in Ear beautiful and naturally accurate, good and price-worthy. World-famous quality toys. Available in toy stores. Brochure L free of charge. Margarete Steiff G.m.b.H., Giengen a. Brenz (Württemberg).

Steiff Triplmobil: The new safe-driving three-wheel auto. Low, steady, great durability. Easy and noiseless run on metal wheels with full rubber tires. Frame-like tread pedals, steel axle with ball bearings. Favorable gear ratio for effortless driving. Elegant lacquer. Pedals adjustable for three to seven-year-olds. Price with freight RM28.00. Brakes and passenger seat on demand. Available everywhere. Color brochure LT free. Margarete Steiff G.m.b.H., Giengen a. Brenz 7 (Württemberg).

1923

Steiff Button in Ear: The mark of quality! Available everywhere. Catalog L free. Margarete Steiff G.m.b.H., Giengen a. Brenz 7 (Württemberg).

1929

For children, sport-proven vehicles—brand "Bärkopf." Safety in fast-riding Steiff Bärkopf Scooter with the quiet, smooth run, solidly built for severe strain. Prices from 3.75 to 10 RM. Lots of pleasure with a new easy-running three-wheel auto Triplmobil. Stressless ride with favorable gear ratio, large metal disc wheels with rubber tires, adjustable seat for three to six-year-olds, fasten-on passenger seat. Store price RM28.00. Available everywhere. Detailed brochures and information free of charge. Margarete Steiff G.m.b.H., Giengen a. Brenz 7 (Württemberg).

1925

Steiff Skiro: The quality scooter. Available everywhere. Brochure L free. Margarete Steiff G.m.b.H., toy factory, Giengen a. Brenz 7 (Württemberg).

1929

It is not bad luck and no disappointment when your child drops its Steiff animal or even falls on it. The soft body will not be damaged and can never hurt or injure. The eyes cannot be lost; they are sewn in and the limbs are permanently fixed.

Steiff Button in Ear animal toys are world-famous for their beauty and quality. They can be given to children without worries. They are always a prized gift. Available in toy stores. Color picture sheet L and information free of charge. Margarete Steiff G.m.b.H., Giengen a. Brenz 7 (Württemberg).

1925

Steiff Button in Ear: The good toy. Available in all toy stores. Brochure L and picture catalog free of charge. Margarete Steiff G.m.b.H., Giengen a. Brenz 7 (Württemberg).

1913

Elephant #1260,2, 60cm (24in) tall, M.36.00
Rocking clown #129, 29cm (11in) tall, M.3.60
Ball #322/9"E, 22cm (9in) tall, M.4.50
Polar bear #1380,2, 80cm (31in) tall, M.56.00
Uniformed soldier #50A, 50cm (20in) tall, M.14.75
Peasant from Dachauer #35, 35cm (14in) tall, M.3.00
Teddy bear #5343,2, 60cm (24in) tall, M.16.00
Lamb #6528,02, 28cm (11in) tall, M.4.00
Above prices are valid only in Germany. Each item carries the trademark "Button in Ear." Available everywhere. No direct sale to private parties. Catalog #20 free. Toy factory Margarete Steiff, G.m.b.H., Giengen-Brenz (Württemberg). Founder and manufacturer of the world-famous "teddy bear." Grand Prix St. Louis 1904 and Brussels 1910.

Steiff Caricature: Schidick 35cm tall. Available in good toy stores. Brochure L and picture illustrations on request. Margarete Steiff, G.m.b.H., Giengen a. Brenz 7 (Württemberg).

1925

Steiff Button in Ear: The good toy. Steiff riding animals have outstanding strength. Available in toy stores. Brochure L and picture illustrations free. Margarete Steiff G.m.b.H., Giengen a. Brenz 7 (Württemberg).

1925

The beloved good toy. Available everywhere. Brochure L and picture catalog free of charge. Margarete Steiff G.m.b.H., Giengen a. Brenz 7 (Württemberg).

1925

Molly, the darling dog for young and old. Available everywhere. Brochure L and picture catalog on request. Margarete Steiff, G.m.b.H., Giengen a. Brenz 7 (Württemberg).

Steiff Button in Ear: The lovely Christmas time is not far off and again one faces the question: "What will we give to our children?" This question is taken care of quickly when you order our catalog #20. It will be mailed to you completely free. You will find wonderful collections of unbreakable toy animals made from felt, velvet, plush, etc., with or without wheels, some with steering, movable, stable or mechanical with natural sounding voices, from a mouse to an elephant. All are accomplished, artistic productions. Each piece carries the "Button in Ear." Grand Prix St. Louis 1904 and Brussels 1910. Available everywhere. Margarete Steiff, G.m.b.H., toy factory, Giengen a. Brenz. Founder and manufacturer of the world-famous "teddy bear." No direct sale to private party.

Felt pig with wheels, #1143, 43cm (17in) tall, M.7.80.
Plush pig, jointed, #8328,2, with patented neck ball joint and automatic voice, sitting, 28cm (11in) tall, M.7.00.
These prices are valid only in Germany.

PART NINE
1913

Felt hare #1122 ex., 22cm (9in) tall, M.4.90
Plush hare #1322 ex., 22cm (9in) tall, M.6.60
Hare #1117 ex., 17cm (7in) tall, M.3.00

Hare #1317 ex., 17cm (7in) tall, M.4.20
Hare #1114 ex., 14cm (6in) tall, M.2.10
Hare #1314 ex., 14cm (6in) tall, M.3.30

Above prices valid only in Germany. Steiff animals are available everywhere. Each item carries the trademark "Button in Ear." Catalog #20 free. Toy factory Margarete Steiff, G.m.b.H., Giengen-Brenz. Founder and manufacturer of the world-famous "teddy bear." Grand Prix St. Louis 1904 and Brussels 1910.

Steiff original chimpanzee with the "Button in Ear." Imitation reproductions of our legally protected production is forbidden by law. Margarete Steiff, G.m.b.H., Toy factory, Giengen-Brenz (Württemberg). Founder and manufacturer of the world-famous "teddy bear." Grand Prix St. Louis 1904 and Brussels 1910. Steiff animals toys are available everywhere. No direct sale to private parties. Catalog #20 free.

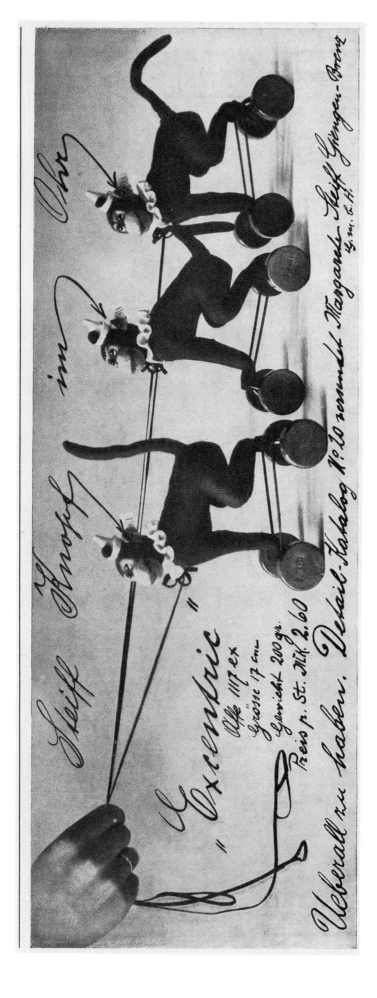

1913

Eccentric monkey #1117 ex., 17cm (7in) tall, 200gm (7oz). Price per each M.2.60. Available everywhere. Detailed catalog #20 sent from Margarete Steiff, Giengen-Brenz.

1914

Steiff original chimpanzees in brown shiny plush on stable wooden wheels with automatic voice. No breakable mechanisms. Pulled with a string. Ask for "Steiff Record-Peter" with the "Button in Ear." Available everywhere. No direct sale to private parties. Manufacture of imitations of our chimpanzees in our legally protected production is forbidden by law.
Record-Peter
#20, 20cm (8in), M.3.75; #25, 25cm (10in), M.4.75; #30, 30cm (12in), M.6.50.
Clown Aujust
#43, 43cm (17in), M.6.50 retail prices for Germany.
Toy factory Margarete Steiff, G.m.b.F., Giengen-Brenz (Württemberg). Founder and manufacturer of the world-famous "teddy bear." Grand Prix St. Louis 1904 and Brussels 1910. Catalog #20 free.

1914

Margarete Steiff, G.m.b.H., Toy factory in Giengen-Brenz (Württemberg). Founder and manufacturer of the world-famous "teddy bear." Each item carries the trademark "Button in Ear." Grand Prix St. Louis 1904 and Brussels 1910. Waddling ducks, felt with colored feathers, on eccentric wooden wheels, which allow the characteristic waddling gait, with the deceiving imitation of duck-quack voice. The funniest toy! Available everywhere. No direct sale to private parties. Catalog #20 free.

#2122,2 ex., 22cm (9in) tall, 30cm (12in) long, 450gm (16oz), retail M.4.50
#2117,2 ex., 17cm (7in) tall, 25cm (10in) long, 290gm (10oz), retail M.3.60
#2114 ex. (with usual squeak voice) 14cm (6in) tall, 20cm (8in) long, 160gm (6oz), retail price M.2.25
These prices valid only in Germany.

1914

Record-Peter in brown shiny plush on stable, self-driving strong wooden wheels and automatic voice. No breakable mechanisms. Pulled on string. Available everywhere.

Record-Peter #20, 20cm (8in), 300gm (11oz), M.3.75
Record-Peter #25, 25cm (10in), 550gm (16oz), M.4.75
Record-Peter #30, 30cm (12in), 820gm (29oz), M.6.50
in elegant packaging. The above prices are valid only in Germany and Austria. No direct sale to private parties. Catalog #20 free. Advertising pamphlets free. Toy factory Margarete Steiff, G.m.b.H., Giengen-Brenz (Württemberg). Founder and manufacturer of the world-famous "teddy-bear." Trademark "Button in Ear." Grand Prix: St. Louis 1904 and Brussels 1910. International building trade award Leipzig 1913: State award from the city of Lubeck.

1913

Spitz #1317/0, 17cm (7in) tall, M.2.00
Shepherd with coat, pipe and shovel, 50cm (20in) tall, M.14.00
Sheep #1522, 22cm (9in) tall, M.2.70
Sheep #1514, 14cm (6in) tall, M.1.20
Sheep #1517, 17cm (7in) tall, M.1.70
These prices valid only in Germany. The whole group is completed as a picture with shepherds, animals, fences and a sheep wagon, (in which all can be packed), together with floor covering 180 by 125cm (71 by 49in), background 180 by 100cm (71 by 39in), M.135.00.
Can be ordered through all toy stores. No direct sale to private parties. Trademark "Button in Ear." Catalog #20 free. Toy factory Margarete Steiff, G.m.b.H., Giengen-Brenz. Founder and manufacturer of the world-famous "teddy bear." Grand Prix St. Louis 1904 and Brussels 1910.

1913

Spitzer Nr. 1317/0. Schäfer, (50 cm gross), Mit Man- (17 cm gross). Mk. 2.— tel, Pfeife u. Schippe Mk. 14.— Die ganze Gruppe komplett wie auf Bild, mit Schäfer, Tieren, Hürden, Schäferkarren (in welchem alles verpackt werden kann), samt bemalten Bodenbelag, 180×125 cm, Hinter- grund 180×100 cm, Mk. 135.—. :: Durch alle Spielwarenhandlungen zu beziehen. :: Kein direkter Versand an Private. :: Schutzmarke „KNOPF IM OHR". :: Katalog Nr. 20 gratis.

Schaf Nr. 1522, (22 cm gross). Mk. 2.70.

Schaf Nr. 1514, (14 cm gross). Mk. 1.20.

(Diese Preise sind nur in Deutschland gültig.)

Schaf. Nr. 1517, (17 cm gross). Mk. 1.70.

Spielwarenfabrik Margarete Steiff, G. m. b. H., Giengen-Brenz. Erfinder und Fabrikanten des weltberühmten „Teddy-Bären". — Grand Prix St. Louis 1904 und Brüssel 1910.

1914

STEIFF: BUTTON IN EAR

Playthings are spread over the whole world.

Back row from left to right:

Polar bear, shiny plush, jointed head and limbs, #8322, 22cm (9in) tall, M.4.75

#8328.2, 28cm (11in) tall, M.7.75

Seal in shiny plush #2317,0, 17cm (7in) tall, M.3.60

Rabbit in wool plush #3514, 14cm (6in) tall, M.2.00

Teddy bear, shiny plush, jointed head and limbs, #5320, 30cm (12in) tall, M.2.80

Spitz dog, shiny plush, jointed head and limbs, #5317, 17cm (7in) tall, M.2.25

Spitz dog on wheels #1317, 17cm (7in) tall, M.2.00

Spitz dog, sitting, #3314, 14cm (6in) tall, M.1.20

Irish Terrier, shiny plush, jointed head/limbs, #5322, 22cm (9in) tall, M.3.75

Eskimo in shiny plush clothes #35, 35cm (14in) tall with ski and stick, M.8.45

Middle row from left to right:

Messenger boy, 35cm (14in), M.4.75

Porter 35cm (14in), M.3.25 or 43cm (17in), M.7.25

Negro footman 35cm (14in), M.8.50

Manfred (50cm) M.15.00

Fanny 50cm (20in), M.15.00

The prices of the dolls and figures do not include accessories such as luggage and the like. Head and limbs of the dolls are jointed.

Front row from left to right:

Lion, shiny plush #1335.2, 35cm (14in) tall, M.12.00

Zebra, plush #1235, 35cm (14in) tall, M.7.50

Golliwog, felt, jointed head and limbs, 28cm (11in) tall, M.2.40

Lion, sitting, shiny plush, jointed head/limbs, #5316, 16cm (6in) tall, M.3.00

Monkey, felt, #4117,0, M.2.00

Lion, shiny plush, jointed head and limbs, #5316, 16cm (6in) tall, M.3.00

Above prices valid only in Germany. No direct sale to private parties. Available in all toy stores. Each item carries the trademark "Button in Ear." Catalog #20 free. Advertisement pamphlets free.

Obere Reihe
(von links nach rechts)

Polarbär aus Glanzplüsch Kopf und Glieder drehbar Nr. 8322 (22 cm gr.) M 4.75 Nr. 8328,2 (28 cm gr.) M 7.75
Seehund aus Glanzplüsch Nr. 2317,0 (17 cm gr.) M 3.60
Hase aus Wollplüsch Nr. 3514 (14 cm gr.) M 2.—
Teddybär aus Glanzplüsch Kopf und Glieder drehbar Nr. 5*20 (30 cm gr.) M. 2.80
Spitzhund aus Glanzp lüsch Kopf und Glieder drehbar Nr. 5317 (17 cm gr.) M 2.25
Spitzhund auf Räder Nr. 1317 (17 cm gr.) M 2.—
Spitzhund, sitzend Nr. 3314 (14 cm gr.) M1.20
Irish Terrier aus Glanzplüsch, Kopf und Glieder drehbar Nr. 5322 (22 cm gr.) M 3.75
Samojede in Glanzplüschanzug Nr. 35 (35 cm gr.) mit Ski und Stock M 8.45

Mittlere Reihe
(von links nach rechts)

Messenger Boy (35 cm) M 4.75
Dienstmann (35 cm) M3.25
do. (43 cm) M 7.25
Negerlakai (35 cm M 8.50
Manfred (50 cm) M 15.—
Fanny (50 cm) M 15.—

(Die Preise der Puppen und Figuren verstehen sich ohne Zubehör, wie Gepäcku. dgl.)
(Kopf und Glieder der Puppen sind drehbar.)

Untere Reihe
(von links nach rechts)

Löwe aus Glanzplüsch Nr. 1335,2 35 cm gr.) M12.—
Zebra aus Plüsch Nr. 1235 (35 cm gr.) M 7.50
Golliwog aus Filz (Kopf und Glieder drehbar) 25 cm gr.) M 2.40
Löwe sitz. aus Glanzplüsch Nr. 3328 (28 cm gr.) M 6.—
Affe aus Filz Nr. 4117,0 M 2.—
Löwe aus Glanzplüsch (Kopf und Glieder drehbar) Nr. 5316.16 cm gr.) M 3.—

Obige Detailpreise haben nur in Deutschland Gültigkeit. Kein direkter Versand an Private. In allen Spielwarenhandlungen zu haben. Jedes Stück trägt als Schutzmarke einen „KNOPF IM OHR".

Katalog Nr. 20 gratis.
Reklame-Marken gratis.

STEIFF · KNOPF IM OHR · SPIELWAREN SIND

ÜBER DIE GANZE WELT VERBREITET

SPIELWARENFABRIK
Margarete STEIFF G. m. b. H.
Giengen - Brenz (Württemberg).

1913

Steiff original chimpanzee with the "Button in Ear."
#5328,2, 28cm (11in) sitting height with growl voice,
M.7.00. Imitation reproductions of our legally protected
productions is forbidden by law. Margarete Steiff,
G.m.b.H., Toy Factory Giengen-Brenz (Württemberg).
Founder and manufacturer of the world-famous "teddy
bear." Grand Prix St. Louis 1904 and Brussels 1910. Steiff
toy animals are available everywhere. No direct sale to
private parties. Catalog #20 free.

STEIFF · KNOPF IM OHR

Steiff Original Schimpanse mit dem „KNOPF IM OHR".
Fabrikationsmässige Nachbildung in unserer ges. geschützt. Ausführung durch rechtskräftiges Urteil verboten.
Margarete Steiff, G. m. b. H., Spielwarenfabrik, Giengen-Brenz (Württemberg).
Erfinder und Fabrikanten des weltberühmten „Teddy"-Bären. Grand Prix St. Louis 1904 und Brüssel 1910.
Steiff Spieltiere sind überall zu haben. Kein direkter Versand an Private. Katalog Nr. 20 gratis.

1915

Steiff original chimpanzee with the "Button in Ear."
#5328,2 (28cm sitting height with growl voice) M.7.00.
Imitation reproductions of our legally protected productions is forbidden by law. Margarete Steiff, G.m.b.H., Toy factory, Geingen-Brenz (Württemberg). Founder and manufacturer of the world-famous "Teddy Bear." Grand Prix St. Louis 1904 and Brussels 1910. Steiff toy animals are available everywhere. No direct sale to private parties. Catalog #20 free.

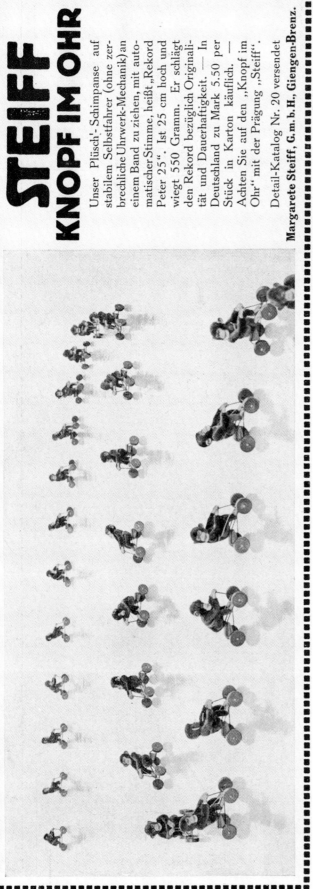

1914

Record-Peter in brown shiny plush on stable, self-driving strong wooden wheels and automatic voice. No breakable mechanisms. Pulled on string. Available everywhere.

Record-Peter #20, 20cm (8in), 300gm (11oz), M.3.75
Record-Peter #25, 25cm (10in), 550gm (16oz), M.4.75
Record-Peter #30, 30cm (12in), 820gm (30oz), M.6.50

in elegant packaging. The above are prices valid only in Germany and Austria. No direct sale to private parties. Catalog #20 free. Advertising pamphlets free. Toy factory Margarete Steiff, G.m.b.H., Giengen-Brenz (Würtemberg). Founder and manufacturer of the world-famous "teddy bear." Trademark "Button in Ear." Grand Prix: St. Louis 1904 and Brussels 1910. International building trade award Leipzig 1913: State award from the city of Lubeck.

Steiff Button in Ear
Our plush chimpanzees on sturdy self-propelled bikes (without breakable motor works) pull on their handles with an automatic voice called "Record Peter 25." He is 25cm tall and weighs 550 grams. He hits the record regarding originality and durability. The price per piece is DM5.5 in Germany. Consider the "Button in Ear" with the impression (embossment) of Steiff.
Send for Detail Catalog #20.

84

STEIFF · KNOPF IM OHR

Bernhardiner Nr.1343,2 (43 cm gross). Nr. 1328 (28 cm gross). Nr. 1335,2 (35 cm gross). Nr. 1350,2 (50 cm gross). Nr. 1360,2 (60 cm gross). Diese Preise sind nur
Mk. 16.—. Mk. 6.75. Mk. 11.50. Mk. 24.50. Mk. 36.—. in Deutschland gültig.
Jedes Stück trägt als Schutzmarke einer „KNOPF IM OHR". Überall zu haben. Kein direkter Versand an Private. Katalog Nr. 20 gratis.
Spielwarenfabrik Margarete Steiff, G. m. b. H., Giengen-Brenz (Württemberg). Erfinder und Fabrikanten des weltberühmten „Teddy-Bären". Grand Prix St. Louis 1904 und Brüssel 1910.

PART TEN
1913

St. Bernard #1343,2 43cm (17cm) tall, M.16.00
 #1328 28cm (11in) tall, M.6.75
 #1335,2 35cm (14in) tall, M.11.50
 #1350,2 50cm (20in) tall, M.24.50
 #1360,2 60cm (24in) tall, M.36.00

These prices valid only in Germany. Each item carries the trademark "Button in Ear." Available everywhere. No direct sale to private parties. Catalog #20 free. Toy factory Margarete Steiff, G.m.b.H., Giengen-Brenz (Württemberg). Founder and manufacturer of the world-famous "teddy bear." Grand Prix St. Louis 1904 and Brussels 1910.

1914

Poodle #1350,2, 50cm (20in) tall, M.22.50
Teddy bear, sitting, #5343,2, 43cm (17in) tall, M.16.00
Elephant #1150,2, 50cm (20in) high, M.19.00
Zottey bear with two-toned voice #1328,0,1, 28cm (11in) tall, M.8.75
Plush ball #320/8E, M.3.50
Steiff toys are indestructible in their construction, artistic in design, precious coverings and childlike. Price list #20 free.
Margarete Steiff, G.m.b.H., Toy factory, Giengen-Brenz (Württemberg).

STEIFF KNOPF IM OHR

Pudel Nr 1350,2 50 cm hoch: M 22.50

Teddy-Bär Nr 5343,2 sitzend 43 cm hoch: M 16.—   Elefant Nr 1150,2 50 cm hoch: M 19.—
Plüsch-Ball Nr 320/8 „E" farbig: M.,3.50   Zottelbär Nr 1328,0.1 28 cm hoch mit Doppelstimme: M 8.75
Steiff-Spielwaren sind unverwüstlich in der Konsruktion, künstlerisch in der Form, wertvoll im Überzug und durchaus kindlich — Preisliste Nr 20 gratis
Margarete Steiff, G. m. b. H., Spielwarenfabrik, Giengen-Brenz (Württemberg)

STEIFF · KNOPF IM OHR

Margarete Steiff, G.m.b.H., Spielwarenfabrik in Giengen-Brenz (Württbg.)
Erfinder und Fabrikanten des weltberühmten „Teddy-Bären".
Jedes Stück trägt als Schutzmarke einen „Knopf im Ohr": Grand Prix St. Louis 1904 u. Brüssel 1910.

Pudel 1335 (35 cm gross)   Ball 315 E   1343,2 (43 cm gr.)   1328 (28 cm gr.)   Ball 312 E   1360,2 (60 cm gr.)   Ball 317 E   1350,2 (50 cm gross)   Ball 310E
M. 9.75   (15 cm) M.2.20   M. 16.50   M. 6.75   (12 cm) M.1.40   M. 32.—   (17 cm) M.2.70   M. 22.50   (10 cm) M. l.—
              Diese Preise sind nur in Deutschland gültig.   Steiff-Spielwaren sind überall zu haben.   Kein direkter Versand an Private.   Katalog No. 20 gratis.

1913

Margarete Steiff, G.m.b.H., Toy factory in Giengen-Brenz (Württemberg). Founder and manufacturer of the world-famous "teddy bear." Each item carries the trademark "Button in Ear." Grand Prix St. Louis 1904 and Brussels 1910.

Poodle 1335, 35cm (14in) tall, M.9.75   Poodle 1360,2, 60cm (24in) tall, M.32.00
Ball 315E, 15cm (6in), M.2.20   Ball 317E, 17cm (7in), M.2.70
Poodle 1343,2, 43cm (17in) tall, M.16.50   Poodle #1350,2, 50cm (20in) tall, M.22.50
Poodle 1328, 28cm (11in) tall, M.6.75   Ball 310E, 10cm (4in), M.1.00
Ball 312E, 12cm (5in), M.1.40
These prices valid only in Germany. Steiff toys are available everywhere. No direct sale to private parties. Catalog #20 free.

Treff

Charly

St. Bernard

Prince

Teddy Baby

Tabby

Zum fröhlichen Spiel

die niedlichen, wuschelweichen Spieltiere Marke

STEIFF · KNOPF IM OHR

Jedes neue Modell, das Sie Ihrem Liebling für seine Steiff-Menagerie schenken, wird ihn noch glücklicher machen. Steiff-Tiere haben wundervollen Ausdruck und sind unverwüstlich.

Zu haben in Spielwarengeschäften. — Farbiger Weihnachts-Katalog L. kostenfrei.

MARGARETE STEIFF G.m.b.H., GIENGEN a. Brenz 7 (Württ.).

1929

For joyful play, get the neat, fuzzy soft toys with quality: Steiff "Button in Ear." Each new model that you give to your darling for his Steiff menagerie will make him even happier. Steiff animals have a wonderful expression and are indestructible. Available in toy stores. Color Christmas catalog L free of charge. Margarete Steiff G.m.b.H., Giengen a. Brenz 7 (Württemberg).

STEIFF · KNOPF IM OHR

Der Brummbär als solideste Spielzeug der Gegenwart aus Glanzplüsch mit Brummstimme, verstärkten Gussrädern und extrastarkem Eisen- und Holzgerippe.

Jedes Stück trägt als Schutzmarke einen „KNOPF IM OHR". Überall zu haben. Kein direkter Versand an Private.

Katalog No. 20 gratis.

Spielwarenfabrik Margarete Steiff, G. m. b. H., Giengen-Brenz (Württemberg). Erfinder und Fabrikanten des weltberühmten „Teddy-Bären".

Grand Prix St. Louis 1904 und Brüssel 1910.

Diese Detailpreise gelten nur für Deutschland.

No. 1328. Höhe inkl. Kopf 28 cm, Länge 37 cm, Gewicht 1,240 kg, Detailpreis M. 8.75 | No. 1335,2. Höhe inkl. Kopf 35 cm, Länge 45 cm, Gewicht 2,340 kg, Detailpreis M. 13.25 | No. 1350,2. Höhe inkl. Kopf 50 cm, Länge 70 cm, Gewicht 5,640 kg, Detailpreis M. 27.— | No. 1322. Höhe inkl. Kopf 22 cm, Länge 30 cm, Gewicht 760 g, Detailpreis M. 5.75 | No. 1317. Höhe inkl. Kopf 17 cm, Länge 23 cm, Gewicht 330 g, Detailpreis M. 3.60 | No. 1343,2. Höhe inkl. Kopf 43 cm, Länge 55 cm, Gewicht 3,940 kg, Detailpreis M. 19.50 | No. 1360,2. Höhe inkl. Kopf 60 cm, Länge 80 cm, Gewicht 8,260 kg, Detailpreis M. 40.—

1913

The riding growler bear, a most durable toy, is made out of shiny plush with growl voice, strengthened cast-iron wheels and extra-strong iron and wooden frame. Each item carries trademark "Button in Ear." Available everywhere. No direct sale to private parties. Catalog #20 free. Toy factory Margarete Steiff, G.m.b.H., Giengen-Brenz (Württemberg). Founder and manufacturer of the world-famous "teddy bear." Grand Prix St. Louis 1904 and Brussels 1910.

Style #	Height, incl. head	Length	Weight (1kg=2.20lb) (1gm=.035oz)	Price
1328	28cm (11in)	37cm (15in)	1.24kg	M.8.75
1335,2	35cm (14in)	45cm (18in)	2.34kg	M.13.25
1350,2	50cm (20in)	70cm (28in)	5.64kg	M.27.00
1322	22cm (9in)	30cm (12in)	.760kg	M.575
1317	17cm (7in)	23cm (9in)	330gr	M.3.60
1343,2	43cm (17in)	55cm (22in)	3.94kg	M.19.50
1360,2	60cm (24in)	80cm (31in)	8.26kg	M.40.00

These prices valid only in Germany.

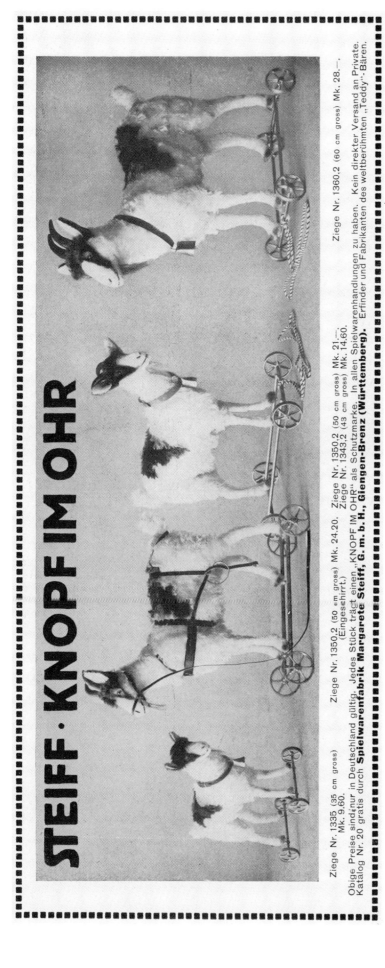

STEIFF · KNOPF IM OHR

Ziege Nr. 1335 (35 cm gross)
Mk. 9.60.

Ziege Nr. 1350,2 (50 cm gross) Mk. 24.20. Ziege Nr. 1350,2 (50 cm gross) Mk. 21.—.
                                  (Eingeschirrt.)

Ziege Nr. 1350,2 (50 cm gross) Mk. 21.—.
Ziege Nr. 1343,2 (43 cm gross) Mk. 14.60.

Ziege Nr. 1360,2 (60 cm gross) Mk. 28.—.

Obige Preise sind nur in Deutschland gültig. Jedes Stück trägt einen „KNOPF IM OHR" als Schutzmarke. In allen Spielwarenhandlungen zu haben. Kein direkter Versand an Private.
Katalog Nr. 20 gratis durch **Spielwarenfabrik Margarete Steiff, G. m. b. H., Giengen-Brenz (Württemberg).** Erfinder und Fabrikanten des weltberühmten „Teddy"-Bären.

1913

Goat #1335, 35cm (14in) tall, M.9.60.
Goat, harnessed #1350,2, 50cm (20in) tall, M.24.20.
Goat #1350,2, 50cm (20in) tall, M.21.00

Goat #1343,2, 43cm (17in) tall, M.14.60
Goat #1360,2, 60cm (24in) tall, M.28.00

Above prices valid only in Germany. Each items carries trademark "Button in Ear." Available in all toy stores. No direct sale to private parties. Catalog #20 free from the toy factory of Margarete Steiff, G.m.b.H., Giegen-Brenz (Württemberg). Founder and manufacturer of the world-famous "teddy bear."

STEIFF KNOPF IM OHR

Winter sport unbreakable dolls, can be dressed and un-
dressed. Each item carries the trademark "Button in Ear."
Gunter 35cm (14in), M.5.60
Hugo 35cm (14in), M.6.30 all in assorted colors
Gisela 35cm (14in), M.6.30
Sigfried 28cm (11in), M.4.70
Sigfried 35cm (14in), M.5.60 all in a white sweater
Silva 28cm (11in), M.5.00
Silva 35cm (14in), M.6.00
Ruth 28cm (11in), M.5.00 both in red sweater
Ruth 35cm (14in), M.6.20
Sleds for dolls size 28 per pair M.0.80
                size 35 per pair M.0.80
Above prices valid only in Germany. Available every-
where. Catalog #20 free. Margarete Steiff G.m.b.H.,
first-class materials cloth animal toys and dolls. Giengen-
Brenz (Württemberg).

STEIFF: BUTTON IN EAR

The beautiful soft *Molly*. Available everywhere. Brochure L and picture catalog free of charge. Margarete Steiff, G.m.b.H., Giengen a. Brenz 7 (Württemberg).

1929

Steiff children's cars: Tretmobil and Tripmobil (Brand Barkopf) are useful elegant vehicles and the wish of every child. Elegant style, an easy and quiet run, proven strong construction, changeable wheels, frame pedals, tooled wheel steering. Brakes, windshield, passenger seat and light on request. The proven quality gives a guarantee for risk-free, healthy fun and year-long pleasure. Available in good toy stores. Vehicle brochure LP on request. Margarete Steiff G.m.b.H., Giengen a. Brenz (Württemberg).

PART ELEVEN

Toy factory Margarete Steiff, G.m.b.H., (Württemberg). Founder and manufacturer of the world-famous "teddy bear." Trademark "Button in Ear." Grand Prix St. Louis 1904 and Brussels 1910. International building trade exhibition Leipzig 1913: State Award. Available everywhere. No direct sales to private parties. Catalog #20 free.

Plush ball #309E, 9cm (4in) diameter, M-.80
Goat with voice #1350,2, 50cm (20in) tall, M.20.00
Record-Teddy with voice, self-driving #25, 25cm (10in) tall, M.4.00
Heiner #35, 35cm (13in) tall, M.5.50
Mouse #2404, M.-.40
Lamb #1517, 17cm (7in) tall, M.1.70
Rosa #35, 35cm (14in) tall, M.6.50
Lamb #1522, 22cm (9in) tall, M.2.70
Donkey, with voice #1250,2, 50cm (20in) tall, M.20.00
Record-Peter, with voice, self-driving #25, 25cm (10in) tall, M.4.75

Hanging on the tree:
Pigeon #6168, M.-.90   Swan #2162, M.-.90
Squirrel #3412, M.1.20   Rabbit #3136, M.-.90
Good-luck pig #1464, M.-.70
These prices valid only in Germany.

1929

It is so nice to play circus with the beautiful and strong-riding animals of the brand Steiff "Button in Ear." The noble style and wonderful characteristics are inspiring. The finest plush felt and strong frame allow an almost unlimited life span. Soundless metal disc wheels with rubber and good handling enable playing in the room without causing damage. Get the world-famous Steiff animals for your child. Available everywhere. Let us show you this catalog. Brochure FL from Margarete Steiff G.m.b.H., Giengen a. Brenz 7 (Württemberg).

1929

Steiff Button in Ear like a beautiful fairy tale. Each Steiff animal brings happiness and joy because children love animals more than anything else. That is why they become friends with these artful play buddies and why this friendship lasts through the whole childhood. Let their first deep impressions of their environment be secured through these beautifully formed animals; surround your darling with a collection of Steiff animals so that they build their fairy tales with all the fantasy of a happy child. Available in toy stores. Color Christmas catalog L and information free of charge. Let us show you the big, main catalog. Margarete Steiff, G.m.b.H., first factory for soft-stuffed animals, Giengen a. Brenz (Württemberg).

97

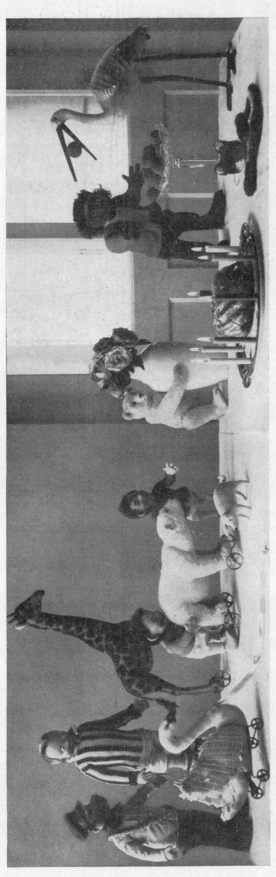

STEIFF · KNOPF IM OHR

Margarete Steiff G. m. b. H., **Giengen-Brenz** (Württbg.) Erfinder und Fabrikanten des weltberühmten „Teddy-Bären". Grand Prix St. Louis 1904 und Brüssel 1910.

| Johann 43 cm gross M. 7.25 | Fussball-Spieler „Kickers" 50 cm gross M.13.50 | Schwan 2122 (22 cm gross) M. 4.20 | Giraffe 1150 (50 cm gross) M. 6.75 | Max .. 30 cm gross M. 2.70 Moritz 30 cm gross M. 2.70 Polarbär 1322 .... M. 5.— (22 cm gross) | Schwein 1408,0 (8 cm gross) M. —.60 | Teddy-Bär 5320 (30 cm gross) M. 2.80 | Golliwog 43 cm gross M. 4.50 | Punchy-Fuchs 317 (17 cm gr.) (Kasperfigur) M. 1.80 | Storch 43 cm gr. M. 5.20 |

Die Preise sind nur in Deutschland gültig. Jedes Stück trägt als Schutzmarke einen „Knopf im Ohr". Überall zu haben. Kein direkter Versand an Private. Katalog No. 20 gratis.

1913

Margarete Steiff G.m.b.H., Giengen-Brenz (Württemberg). Founder and manufacturer of the world-famous "teddy bear." Grand Prix St. Louis 1904 and Brussels 1910.

Johann 43cm (17in) tall, M.7.25
Soccer player *Kickers* 50cm (20in) tall, M.13.50
Swan #2122, 22cm (9in) tall, M.4.20
Giraffe #1150, 50cm (20in) tall, M.6.75
Max 30cm (12in) tall, M.2.70
Moritz 30cm (12in) tall, M.2.70

Polar bear #1322, 22cm (9in) tall, M.5.00
Pig #1408,0, 8cm (3in) tall, M.-.60
Teddy bear #3520, 30cm (12in) tall, M.2.80
Golliwog 43cm (17in) tall, M.4.50
Punchy Fox #317, 17cm (7in) tall, M.1.80
Stork 43cm (17in) tall, M.5.20

These prices valid only in Germany. Each item carries trademark "Button in Ear." Available everywhere. No direct sale to private parties. Catalog #20 free.

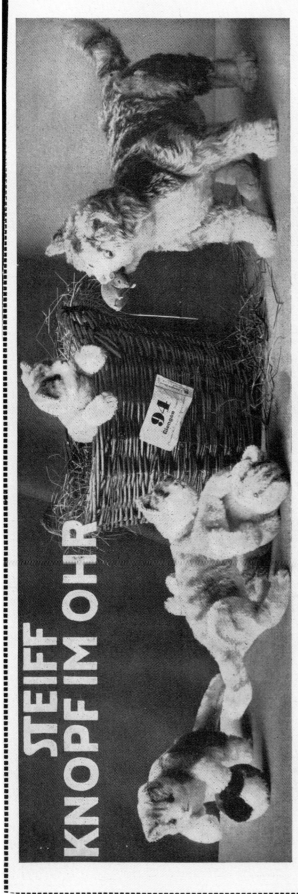

STEIFF
KNOPF IM OHR

Weichgestopfte Katzen aus langhaarigem, prachtvollem Ganzplüsch in grau-weißer Farbe, mit drehbarem Kopf, beweglichen Gliedern und vorzüglich nachgeahmter Katzenstimme.
No. 5322,2 (22 cm) M. 4.50 No. 5328,2 (28 cm) M. 7.25 No. 5335,2 (35 cm) M. 10.—
Plüsch-Ball No. 307 E (7 cm) M. —.55 Überall zu haben. — Jedes Stück trägt als Schutzmarke einen „KNOPF IM OHR". Kein direkter Versand an Private. — Katalog No. 20 gratis.
Spielwarenfabrik Margarete Steiff, G. m. b. H, Giengen a. **Brenz (Württemberg).** — Erfinder und Fabrikanten des weltberühmten „Teddy-Bären". — Grand Prix St. Louis 1904 und Brüssel 1910.

1913

Soft stuffed cats made from long-haired, magnificent shiny plush in gray-white color with movable head, jointed limbs and an excellently imitated cat voice.

#5322,2, 22cm (9in), M.4.50   Felt mouse #2104, 4cm (2in), M.-.80
Plush ball #307E, 7cm (3in), M.-.55   #5335,2, 35cm (14in), M.10.00
#5328,2, 28cm (11in), M.7.25

Available everywhere. Each item carries the trademark "Button in Ear." No direct sale to private parties. Catalog #20 free. Toy factory Margarete Steiff, G.m.b.H, Giengen a. Brenz (Württemberg). Founder and manufacturer of the world-famous "teddy bear." Grand Prix St. Louis 1904 and Brussels 1910.

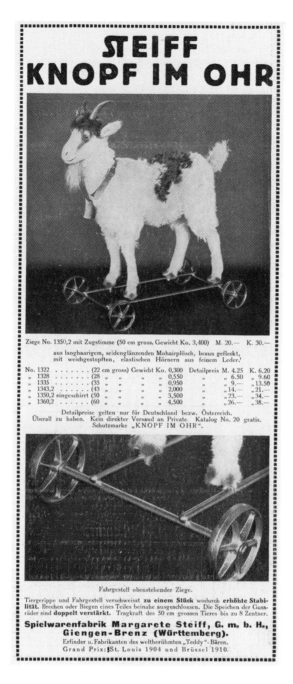

1913

Goat #1350,2 with pull voice, 50cm (20in) tall, 3.4kg (7lb), M.20.00 made of long-haired, silken mohair plush, brown-speckled, with soft-stuffed resilient horns made of fine leather.

#1322	22cm (9in) tall	.30kg (.66lb)	M.4.25
#1328	28cm (22in) tall	.55kg (1lb)	M.6.50
#1335	35cm (14in) tall	.95kg (2lb)	M.9.00
#1343,2	43cm (17in) tall	2kg (4lb)	M.14.00
#1350,2	50cm (20in) tall	3.5kg (6lb)	M.23.00
#1360,2	60cm (24in) tall	4.5kg (10lb)	M.26.00

Retail prices valid only in Germany and Austria. Available everywhere. No direct sale to private parties. Catalog #20 free. Trademark "Button in Ear."

Frame and wheels of the above goat. The animal frame and wheel frame are welded into a unit contributing to increased stability. The spokes of the cast iron wheels are doubly reinforced. Carrying capacity of this 50cm (20in) high animal up to 400kg (882lb).

Toy factory Margarete Steiff, G.m.b.H., Giengen-Brenz (Württemberg). Founder and manufacturer of the world-famous "teddy bear." Grand Prix St. Louis 1904 and Brussels 1910.

STEIFF · KNOPF IM OHR

„Rekord-Teddy-Bären" No. 25 aus hellbraunem Glanzplüsch. Auf stabilem Selbstfahrer mit starken Holz-rädern. Keine zerbrechliche Mechanik. Nur am Band zu ziehen. Automatische Stimme. Höhe 25 cm. Länge 23 cm. Gewicht 540 gr. Detailpreis in Deutschland M. 4.—, in Österreich K. 6.— p. St. in Karton.

Überall zu haben. Kein direkter Versand an Private. Schutzmarke „Knopf im Ohr". Katalog No. 20 gratis.

Spielwarenfabrik Margarete Steiff, G. m. b. H., Giengen-Brenz (Württemberg).
Erfinder und Fabrikanten des weltberühmten „Teddy-Bären".
Grand Prix; St. Louis 1904 und Brüssel 1910. Internationale Baufach-Ausstellung, Leipzig 1913: Staatspreis.

PART TWELVE
1914

Record-Teddy-Bear in light brown shiny plush #25. Stable self-driver with strong wooden wheels. No breakable mechanisms. Pullable on string. Automatic voice. 25cm (10in) tall, 23cm (9in) long. Weighs 540gm (19oz). Retail price in Germany M.4.00. Each piece in box. Available everywhere. No direct sale to private parties. Trademark "Button in Ear." Catalog #20 free. Toy factory Margarete Steiff, G.m.b.H., Giengen-Brenz (Württemberg). Founder and manufacturer of the world-famous "teddy bear." Grand Prix St. Louis 1904 and Brussels 1910. International building trade exhibition Leipzig 1913: State award.

The beautiful gift for a child or lady.
Steiff animals are beautiful, good and
price-worthy. Available everywhere.
Brochure L free of charge. Margarete
Steiff G.m.b.H., Giengen a. Brenz 7
(Württemberg).

STEIFF KNOPF IM OHR

A whole world of animals in a room beautiful and expressive, true-to-nature and life-like with the world-famous animals of Margarete Steiff. You will enjoy the deep and lasting friendship of your darling with his Steiff animals. A four-legged companion with the symbol "Button in Ear" takes no care and is no less loyal, so beautiful and soft, so right to cuddle and play with: the ideal playmate. Available everywhere. Detailed brochure L free of charge. Margarete Steiff G.m.b.H., Giengen a. Brenz 7 (Württemberg).

Steiff-Original-Schimpansen in farbigem Filz oder Glanzplüsch auf stabilem Selbstfahrer mit starken Holzrädern und automatischer Stimme. Keine zerbrechliche Mechanik! Nur am Band zu ziehen. Ueberall zu haben. Verlangen Sie „Steiff-Rekord-Peter" mit dem „Knopf im Ohr". Die fabrikationsmässige Nachbildung unseres Schimpansen in der uns ges. gesch. Ausführung ist durch rechtskräftiges Urteil verboten.

Spielwarenfabrik Margarete Steiff, G. m. b. H., Giengen a. Brenz (Württemberg). Erfinder und Fabrikanten des weltberühmten „Teddy-Bären". Grand Prix St. Louis 1904 und Brüssel 1910.

Rekord-Peter No. 25, in schwarz. Glanzplüsch, 25 cm hoch, Gewicht 550 gr **M. 4.75.**
Rekord-Peter No. 25, in gelbem Glanzplüsch, 25 cm hoch, Gewicht 550 gr **M. 4.75.**
Rekord-Peter No. 125, in rotem Filz, 25 cm hoch, Gewicht 540 gr **M. 4.25.**
Rekord-Peter No. 20, in braunem Glanzplüsch, 20 cm hoch, Gewicht 300 gr **M. 3.75.**
Rekord-Peter No. 120, in rotem Filz, 20 cm hoch, Gewicht 300 gr **M. 3.75.**
Rekord-Peter No. 20, in blauem Glanzplüsch, 25 cm hoch, Gewicht 300 gr **M. 3.75.**

Jedes Stück wird in elegantem Karton verkauft.   Kein direkter Versand an Private.   Katalog No. 20 gratis.   Obige Detailpreise gelten nur in Deutschland.

1913

Steiff original chimpanzee in felt color or shiny plush with stable self-drivers, strong wooden wheels and automatic voices. No breakable mechanisms. Pulled with a string. Available everywhere. Ask for "Steiff Record-Peter" with "Button in Ear." Manufacturing imitations of our legally protected product is forbidden by law. Toy factory Margarete Steiff, G.m.b.H., Giengen a. Brenz (Württemberg). Founder and manufacturer of the world-famous "teddy bear." Grand Prix St. Louis 1904 and Brussels 1910.

Record-Peter, black shiny plush, 25cm (10in) tall, 550gm (16oz), M.4.75.
Record-Peter, yellow shiny plush, 25cm (10in) tall, 500gm (16oz), M.4.75.
Record-Peter, red felt #120, 20cm (8in) tall, 300gm (11oz), M.4.25.
Record-Peter, brown shiny plush #20, 20cm (8in) tall, 300gm (11oz), M.3.75.
Record-Peter, red felt #120, 20cm (8in) tall, 300gm (11oz), M.3.25.
Record-Peter, blue shiny plush #20, 25cm (10in) tall, 300gm (11oz), M.3.75.
Each item packed in an elegant box. No direct sale to private parties. Catalog #20 free. Above prices valid only in Germany.

1913

Bear in brown shiny plush, 28cm (11in) tall, movable head, on extra strong iron wheels with leather collar and nickel-plated chain. #1328 M.8.75

Teddy bears in white, light or dark brown, shiny plush with jointed head and limbs and growl voice. Stands 35cm (14in) tall. #5325,2 each item M.5.20. Available everywhere. No direct sale to private parties. Above prices valid only in Germany. Catalog #20 free. Toy factory Margarete Steiff, G.m.b.H., Giengen a. Brenz (Württemberg). Founder of the world-famous "teddy bear." Trademark "Button in Ear." Grand Prix St. Louis 1904 and Brussels 1910.

Record-Peter in brown shiny plush or in red felt, stable, self-driving, with strong wooden wheels and automatic voice. No breakable mechanisms. Pullable on a string.
Retail prices for Germany:
In shiny plush:

#20	300gm (11oz)	20cm (8in) tall	M.3.75
#25	550gm (16oz)	25cm (10in) tall	M.4.75
#30	820gm (29oz)	30cm (12in) tall	M.6.50

In felt:

#120	300gm (11oz)	20cm (8in) tall	M.3.25
#125	550gm (16oz)	25cm (10in) tall	M.4.25

Available everywhere. No direct sale to private parties. Catalog #20 free. Margarete Steiff, G.m.b.H., toy factory Giengen-Brenz (Württemberg). Founder and manufacturer of the world-famous "teddy bear."

STEIFF KNOPF IM OHR

Rekord-Peter

aus braunem Glanz-
plüsch, beziehgsw.
rotem Filz, auf sta-
bilem Selbstfahrer
mit starken Holz-
rädern, mit auto-
matischer Stimme

Keine zerbrech-
liche Mechanik

Nur an einem
Bande zu ziehen

Detailpreise für
Deutschland:

Aus Glanzplüsch

Nr	Gewicht	Höhe	M
20	300 gr	20 cm	3.75
25	550 "	25 "	4.75
30	820 "	30 "	6.50

Aus Filz

Nr	Gewicht	Höhe	M
120	300 gr	20 cm	3.25
125	550 "	25 "	4.25

Detailpreise für
Oesterreich:

Aus Glanzplüsch

Nr	Gewicht	Höhe	Kr
20	300 gr	20 cm	5.50
25	550 "	25 "	7.—
30	820 "	30 "	9.60

Aus Filz

Nr	Gewicht	Höhe	Kr
120	300 gr	20 cm	4.80
125	550 "	25 "	6.20

Ueberall zu haben

Kein direkter Ver-
sand an Private

Katalog Nr 20 gratis

**Margarete
Steiff**

G. m. b. H.

Spielwarenfabrik

Giengen-Brenz
(Württemberg)

Erfinder u. Fabrikanten
des weltberühmten
Teddy-Bären

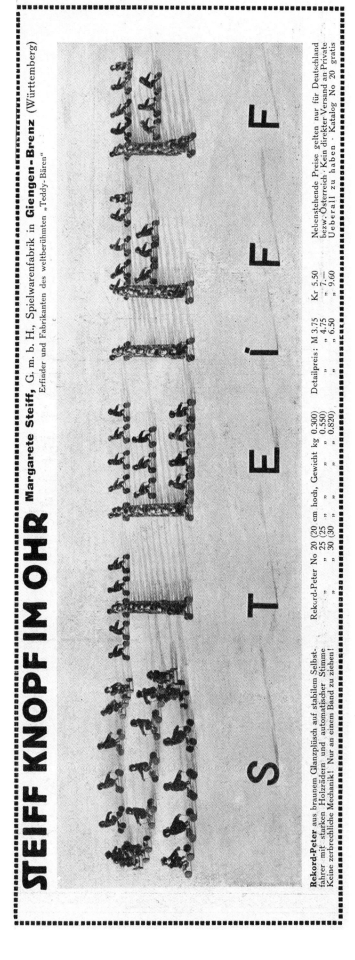

STEIFF KNOPF IM OHR

Margarete Steiff, G. m. b. H., Spielwarenfabrik in **Giengen-Brenz** (Württemberg)
Erfinder und Fabrikanten des weltberühmten „Teddy-Bären"

Rekord-Peter aus braunem Glanzplüsch auf stabilem Selbstfahrer mit starken Holzrädern und automatischer Stimme. Keine zerbrechliche Mechanik! Nur an einem Band zu ziehen!

Rekord-Peter	No 20	(20 cm hoch,	Gewicht kg 0.300)	Detailpreis: M 3.75	Kr 5.50
"	25	(25 " "	" 0.550)	" 4.75	" 7.—
"	30	(30 " "	" 0.820)	" 6.50	" 9.60

Nebenstehende Preise gelten nur für Deutschland bezw. Österreich · Kein direkter Versand an Private Ueberall zu haben · Katalog No 20 gratis

1914

Margarete Steiff, G.m.b.H., Toy factory in Giengen-Brenz (Württemberg). Founder and manufacturer of the world-famous "teddy bear."

Record-Peter in brown shiny plush, stable and self-driving, with strong wooden wheels and automatic voice. No breakable mechanisms. Pullable on a string.

#20	300gm (11oz)	20cm (8in) tall	M.3.75
#25	550gm (16oz)	25cm (10in) tall	M.4.75
#30	820gm (29oz)	30cm (12in) tall	M.6.50

Accompanying prices valid only in Germany or Austria. Available everywhere. Catalog #20 free.

STEIFF·KNOPF IM OHR

Plüsch-Reh Nr. 1250. (50 cm gross.) Mk. 13.50.   Filz-Reh Nr. I1150. (50 cm gross.) Mk. 12.30.   Nr. 1160. (60 cm gross.) Mk. 16.50.   Plüsch-Reh Nr. 1260. (60 cm gross.). Mk. 18.50.
Obige Preise sind nur in Deutschland gültig. Jedes Stück trägt einen „KNOPF IM OHR" als Schutzmarke. In allen Spielwarenhandlungen zu haben. Kein direkter Versand an Private.
Katalog Nr. 20 versendet gratis **Spielwarenfabrik Margarete Steiff, G. m. b. H., Giengen-Brenz** (Württemberg). Erfinder und Fabrikanten des weltberühmten „Teddy"-Bären.

1913

Plush deer	#1250	50cm (20in) tall	M.13.50
Felt deer	#1150	50cm (20in) tall	M.12.30
Felt deer	#1160	60cm (24in) tall	M.16.50
Plush deer	#1260	60cm (24in) tall	M.18.50

Above prices applicable only in Germany. Each item carries trademark "Button in Ear." Available in all toy stores. No direct sale to private parties. Catalog #20 sent free of charge. Toy factory Margarete Steiff, G.m.b.H., Giengen-Brenz (Württemberg). Founder and manufacturer of the world-famous "teddy bear."

Toy factory Margarete Steiff, G.m.b.H., Geingen-Brenz (Württemberg). Founder and manufacturer of the world-famous "Teddy Bear."

Drill soldiers 43cm tall each item M.5.80
Corporal 43cm tall M.7.70
Boots per pair M.1.20
Cloth soldier 43cm tall M.7.40
Fox terrier #1414/0. 14cm tall M.1.30
Major 43cm tall M.8.00
Guard with rifle 43cm tall M.10.50
Guard house 62cm tall M.6.75
Lieutenant 45cm tall M.5.00
Price for the complete barracks with background M.115.00. Soldiers with "Button in Ear" are available everywhere. No direct shipment to private parties. Catalog #20 free.

111

STEIFF KNOPF IM OHR

Reh in Plüsch Nr. 1250.
(50 cm gross; Gewicht kg 3,500.)
Deutscher Detailpreis M. 13.50.

Margarete Steiff, G. m. b. H., Spielwarenfabrik,
Giengen-Brenz (Württemberg).

Reh in Filz Nr. 1150.
(50 cm gross; Gewicht kg 3,500.)
Deutscher Detailpreis M. 11.—.

Erfinder und Fabrikanten des weltberühmten „Teddy-Bären".
Schutzmarke „KNOPF IM OHR". — Überall zu haben. — Katalog Nr. 20 gratis.

1913

Margarete Steiff, G.m.b.H., Giengen-Brenz (Württemberg).

Founder and manufacturer of the world-famous "teddy bear." Trademark "Button in Ear." Available everywhere. Catalog #20 free.

Plush deer #1250, 50cm (20in) tall, weighs 3.5kg (10lb). German retail price M.13.50.

Felt deer #1150, 50cm (20in) tall, weighs 3.5kg (10lb). German retail price M.11.00.

1913

Spiral plane kits
a) with 2 wings

Item wt./ kilos	Wing span/cm	Avg.carry capacity/kilos	Price each/ Germany
0.310	120/2	0.7	M.4.40
0.450	150/2	1.0	M.6.00
0.610	180/2	2.0	M.7.80
1.070	210/2	4.0	M.10.00
1.320	240/2	6.0	M.12.75
1.790	270/2	8.0	M.14.75
2.410	300/2	10.0	M.18.00
2.700	330/2	20.0	M.22.75
3.900	360/2	30.0	M.26.25
b) with 3 wings			
.730	180/3	2.0	M.10.00
1.140	210/3	4.0	M.12.30
1.510	240/3	6.0	M.15.00
1.850	270/3	10.0	M.18.00
2.500	300/3	18.0	M.22.25
3.180	330/3	35.0	M.25.50
3.900	360/3	50.0	M.33.00

These prices are for sack cloth and 2 reserve rods. Each spiral plane includes a detailed illustrated description.

Photographed from a 200 meter height from a Steiff spiral plane-kite. #360/3 M.33.00 and Steiff stand M.21.00. At the international kite flying competition in Spa (Belgium) in August 1912 this same kite and stand won a total of 2700 francs in prize money.

Spiral plane kite #180/2. (180cm high and broad with 2 wings.) M.7.80. Metal spool with 250 hemp line (tested) M.6.60. Special kite list free from Margarete Steiff, G.m.b.H., Giengen-Brenz 20. Steiff spiral planes available in toy stores all over the world.

Steiff Button in Ear
Toy Factory Margarete Steiff
Founder and creator of the world renowned "teddy bears." Available everywhere. Trademark — Button in Ear. Catalog #20 free of charge. No direct mail orders. Steiff "teddy bears" mark — "Button in Ear" of shiny plush, white bright and dark brown. Head and limbs are rotatable. In sizes from 10 to 15cm and price ranges from DM.75 to 56.—.

PART THIRTEEN

It was Betty who delivered the invitation, in such solemn fashion that the Teddy Bears all sat them down on the bed to consider. As Betty went on to explain they were all attention; even Baloo, the Indifferent One, cocked his stubby ears and leaned forward until Ab, his small charge, nearly toppled over on his nose. Of course they would go; but *what* should they wear? Peter — big, tawny Peter — thought his pink neck-ribbon would be more becoming than his blue; yet he did so love blue. Little Scrub, sitting beside his beloved Barbara, wondered if it would be quite proper to wear his blue jeans. You can't imagine how excited they were; one isn't invited to a tea party every day — that is, if one is a Teddy Bear. Not that they cared about the tea, but they did hope there would be *plenty* of honey.

Now, a tea-party means a rehearsal of one's manners. At the thought most of the Teddy Bears scampered away and pretended to be busily washing their paws (Betty never interrupted them in that!). Ab and Ba, the twins, climbed onto Baloo's lap and declared *they'd* be *very* good. But Peter had a request to make: Might he sit at the head of the table? Betty said he might if he could find the head of a round table.

Well, the party was a success. Each Teddy Bear wore a fresh neckribbon and his jauntiest manner; except Scrub, who *would* keep on his blue jeans, so they made him sit by the window by himself. Peter was wonderful and Betty couldn't eat for admiration of him. As there weren't chairs enough to go around some perched on the tops; and though, at this dizzy height, they couldn't manage tea-cups, they *all* had lots of honey; till even Peter lay back sleepy and satisfied.
Page is hand colored

116

The Teddy Bears' Tea-Party

By Lucy Leffingwell Cable

Photographs by Mary H. Northend

IT WAS Betty who delivered the invitation, in such solemn fashion that the Teddy Bears all sat them down on the bed to consider. As Betty went on to explain they were all attention; even Baloo, the Indifferent One, cocked his stubby ears and leaned forward until Ab, his small charge, nearly toppled over on his nose. Of course they would go; but *what* should they wear? Peter—big, tawny Peter—thought his pink neck-ribbon would be more becoming than his blue; yet he did so love blue. Little Scrub, sitting beside his beloved Barbara, wondered if it would be quite proper to wear his blue jeans. You can't imagine how excited they were; one isn't invited to a tea-party every day—that is, if one is a Teddy Bear. Not that they cared about the tea, but they did hope there would be *plenty* of honey.

NOW, a tea-party means a rehearsal of one's manners. At that thought most of the Teddy Bears scampered away and pretended to be busily washing their paws (Betty never interrupted them in that!). Ab and Ba, the twins, climbed into Baloo's lap and declared they'd be *very* good. But Peter had a request to make: *Might* he sit at the head of the table? Betty said he might if he could find the head of a round table.

WELL, the party was a success. Each Teddy Bear wore a fresh neck-ribbon and his jauntiest manner; except Scrub, who *would* keep on his blue jeans, so they made him sit in the window by himself. Peter was wonderful and Betty couldn't eat for admiration of him. As there weren't chairs enough to go around some perched on the tops; and though, at this dizzy height, they couldn't manage tea-cups, they *all* had lots of honey; till even Peter lay back sleepy and satisfied.

Black and white English postcard from 1909.

Sepia postcard.

Sepia postcard from England.

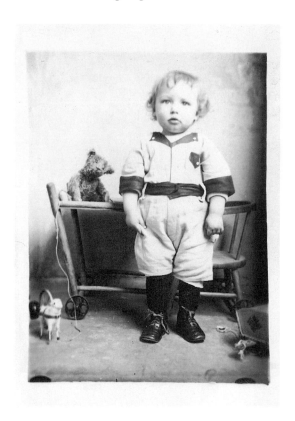

Sepia postcard without any mark of origin.

Sepia postcard from England marked 1910.

Sepia postcard printed in England.

Greeting
—
Keep a little bare spot
In your heart for me:
You'll find me faithful
As Teddy B.

COPYRIGHT 1907. HELEN L. McCARTHY

Sepia postcard copyrighted 1910.

Sepia postcard.

One of the Blues.

Postmarked 1910, this postcard features a Steiff doll
and is titled "One of the Blues."

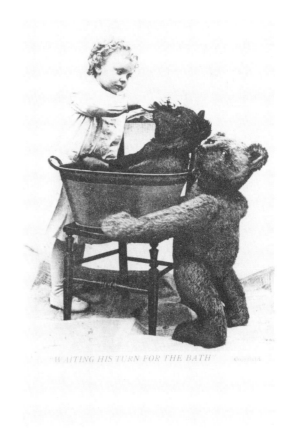

WAITING HIS TURN FOR THE BATH

Sepia postcard made in England.

Nach einem photogr Bildnis von Karl Schenker, Berlin.

WANDA TREUMANN

Sepia postcard of Wanda Treumann and her Steiff
teddy.

To Wish You A Merry Christmas.

Wishing You Joy.

May Christmas-
-tide be
a season bright-
of
happiness
and
heart's delight.

Sepia postcard printed in England.

DORRIT WEIXLER

Sepia postcard of Dorrit Weixler and her bear.

Hand colored postcard of a child with a bisque doll and a Steiff teddy.

Black and white postcard of a four-year-old and her bear.

Hand colored postcard.

Eva May

Verlag „ROSS", Berlin SW 66

Sepia postcard of Eva May and her teddy.

Sepia photograph of an elegant little boy and a bear.

Hand colored postcard from France, dated 1927.

Sepia postcard showing Prince Alexander Ferdinand.

122

Sepia postcard of Miss Gabrielle Ray and two Steiff dolls.

Hand tinted postcard.

Black and white postcard is one of a series.

Postmarked 1919, this card shows a variety of toys of the period.

Hand colored Christmas postcard from 1915.

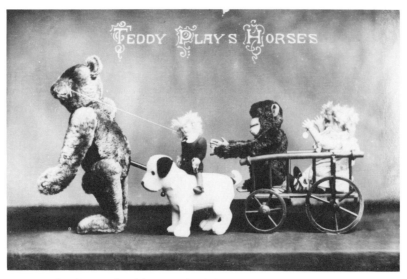

Sepia card with wonderful Steiff toys and dolls.

Black and white postcard of British manufacture.

Hand colored and postmarked 1925, a variety of Steiff toys are shown in a woodland setting.

Sepia card of a child and teddy.

"Here I come on Christmas Day,
Don't I look like Santa Claus?"
So says happy Teddy-bear,
Pulling with his furry paws,

Such a pretty little sleigh
Full of Toys all bright and new,
And the dear wee puppy-dog
Bringing lots of fun to You.

Fond Love and Christmas Greetings.

Sepia postcard with a Steiff teddy pulling a sled.

Sepia photograph of a child with a pull-toy cat and a teddy.

Sepia photograph of a small boy and his bear.

Sepia photograph of two children with a teddy.

Black and white of a boy and teddy.

Color postcard with a gilded and embossed border, printed in Saxony.